Fact Book
on Aging

Fact Book on Aging

Elizabeth Vierck

ABC-CLIO

Santa Barbara, California
Oxford, England

Library of Congress Cataloging-in-Publication Data

Vierck, Elizabeth, 1945–
    Fact book on aging / Elizabeth Vierck.
        p. cm.
    Includes bibliographical references.
    1. Aged—United States—Handbooks, manuals, etc. 2. Old age—
United States—Handbooks, manuals, etc. 3. Aging—United States—
Handbooks, manuals, etc. 4. Retirement—United States—Handbooks,
manuals, etc. I. Title
    HQ 1064.U5V494 1990   305.26'0973—dc20   90-34667

ISBN 0-87436-284-9 (alk. paper)

97 96 95 94 93 92   10 9 8 7 6 5 4 3 2

ABC-CLIO, Inc.
130 Cremona Drive, P.O. Box 1911
Santa Barbara, California 93116-1911

Clio Press Ltd.
55 St. Thomas' Street
Oxford, OX1 1JG, England

This book is printed on acid-free paper ⊗.
Manufactured in the United States of America

For Craig

Contents

Chapter 4
Work and Retirement, 24

Chapter 5
Seniors and Money, 32

Chapter 6
Marital Status, Living Arrangements, and Family, 47

Chapter 7
Education and Native Language, 55

Chapter 8
Housing, 59

Preface

One of the catchy phrases that is used over and over again to describe the demographic revolution facing our county is "America is aging." However, America is not just aging. It *has* aged. Consider just three startling facts:

- Ten years have been added to the median age of the U.S. population since 1900
- Two-thirds of all the seniors in the world who have ever lived are alive today
- America's seniors now outnumber the entire population of Canada

As we face this demographic revolution there is a need for readily accessible, timely facts on the status of seniors, their attitudes, beliefs, and desires. The *Fact Book on Aging* is designed to fill this need. With over 1,500 statistical "one-liners" and a practical, detailed index, there is no other publication like this one that provides quick access to a wide range of facts on aging.

The *Fact Book* is written for a broad audience of aging professionals, information specialists, researchers, analysts, writers, and others concerned with aging. It includes information from a wide scope of sources including the U.S. Bureau of the Census, Bureau of Labor Statistics, Department of Education, Department of Health and Human Services, National Center for Health Statistics, Health Care Financing Administration, Department of Justice, Congressional Research Service, U.S. Senate Special Committee on Aging, U.S. House of Representatives Committee on Ways and Means, American Association of Retired Persons (AARP), Administration on Aging, National Institute on Aging, *Older Americans Reports,* and *Mature Market Reports.*

The *Fact Book* covers subjects ranging from the demographics of aging to achievements made at an advanced age. It includes such topics as: retirement and work; income and poverty; volunteering and community involvement; leisure time, travel, and religion; crimes against and by seniors; health status of seniors; use of health services; long-term care; paying for health care; what seniors and other adults think about aging-related issues; the senior market; federal outlays; major legislation benefitting seniors; and the world's senior population.

The range of topics covered offers a view of the tremendous impact that aging has on all aspects of society and that society, in turn, has on aging. To maximize accessibility to the sheer bulk of material, this book is organized into 20 chapters of varying length covering discrete subject areas. Facts related to a particular topic, such as long-term care, are grouped together within chapters. However, a quick glance at the index reveals that, frequently, related information also can be found in other chapters. For example, while Chapter 15 covers long-term care, related facts, such as public and private spending for long-term care, appear elsewhere.

As a general rule the *Fact Book* covers data for persons over age 65. However, when data for this age group are not available, statistics may include 55- or 60-plus persons. Persons over age 65 are referred to as seniors, older persons, or the older population. When discrete age groups are discussed, such as the youngest-old or oldest-old, they are referred to by chronological age.

Every effort has been made to include complete sources for all 1,500-plus points of data in this book. Each one-sentence fact is keyed to an end-of-chapter note that lists the author of the source, the year of the publication, and a page number. When more than one publication from an author or institution is cited in the bibliography at the end of the book, the note also includes an abbreviated title. In order to obtain the complete reference the reader should look in the bibliography at the end of the book.

Two caveats regarding the end-of-chapter notes must be mentioned for clarity. First, the *Fact Book on Aging* sometimes cites *Aging America*, which the author recently revised for the U.S. Senate Special Committee on Aging. *Aging America* is published every two years in two versions. The first version is issued as a Senate Special Committee on Aging committee print. A second, sturdier, color version is jointly produced and printed by the U.S. Senate Special Committee on Aging, the American Association of Retired Persons (AARP), the Administration on Aging (AOA), and the Federal Council on Aging. All endnotes in this book refer to page numbers in the first printing of the committee print version only.

Second, to maintain the integrity of the data, an attempt has been made to use the specific terms employed by specific data sources. Therefore, terminology is not always consistent throughout the document. For example, when describing similar populations, the Social Security Administration refers to "consumer units" while the U.S. Bureau of the Census refers to "households." Where I have anticipated that there might be confusion regarding the terms used, an explanation has been included in the relevant notes.

Finally, this book is designed as a quick source to what we presently know about how America has aged. The *Fact Book on Aging* is also, I hope, a contribution toward preparing for the future—as the older population doubles in size over the next four decades.

Acknowledgments

This book is the result of eight years of compiling data on aging. I would like to thank the following people who have been instrumental in that process: Cyndy Taeuber, John Rother, Larry Atkins, Don Fowles, Tom Gabe, Connie Swank, Chris Jennings, Beth Soldo, Korbin Liu, Ken Manton, Mary Grace Kovar, Joan Van Nostrand, Jeanne Griffith, and Craig Boyle. I would also like to express regret that Linda Harootyan, who had planned to coauthor this book, was not able to do so. Her insights and enthusiasm in the planning stages were invaluable to the project. Special thanks also go to Yale and Jane Huffman and Craig Boyle for their help with "The Typical Senior." I would also like to thank the staffs of the following agencies for their help in supplying information and analysis: the U.S. Bureau of the Census, the National Center for Health Statistics, the Department of Labor, the Congressional Research Service, the Employee Benefit Research Institute, and *Mature Market Report*. Last, but not least, I am grateful to a number of people at ABC-CLIO—to my editor, Heather Cameron, for her sound guidance; to Laurie Brock who offered excellent advice in the developmental stages of the project; and to Martha Whitt and John Graham for their hard work on two versions of the final draft.

The Typical Senior

Who is the typical senior? Prior to writing this book I had resisted responding to this question because the answer could be but a sketch—leaving much of the texture and ambiance in the paint box and off the canvas. If I make the statement that the "typical" older family had an income of $21,705 in 1988, for example, I overlook the reality of 85-year-old Corrine Gable of Mobile, Alabama, who takes in laundry in her shack and who, like 57 percent of black women on their own, lives in bleak poverty. Or the Rotondos, who have spent their entire life savings for care for Mrs. Rotondo, who has Alzheimer's disease. For that matter, I also slight multimillionaire Albert Myers, who is starting yet another business at age 75.

Nevertheless, since 1981 when I first started compiling statistics on age and aging, I have received many requests for a synopsis of what these numbers mean. In other words, when you put all the numbers together, what is the typical senior like? What are his or her circumstances? Therefore, I feel compelled to try to summarize these statistics for those readers who are interested. The following, then, is an attempt to sketch a portrait of the typical senior—albeit with the limitations of painting an abstract by numbers. It is based on the information presented in this book.

Every Eighth American

Let me introduce you to the typical senior today. Because senior women outnumber men three to two, she is a woman. For convenience's sake we will call her Mrs. Perkins. Now 72 years old, she was born in the decade when Wilson was President. Her experience spans the waltz, the two-step, and the twist. She has suffered through full-length skirts and bikinis, and is presently enjoying the era of "anything goes" in fashion. She has lived through three wars; the stock market crash of 1929 and the Great Depression; "red fever" and the building and tearing down of the Berlin wall; the

Model T and walks on the moon; and the introduction of talkies, the radio, television, the computer, and fax machines.

When Mrs. Perkins was born only 1 in 25 Americans was over age 65. Today seniors are a major force in society—representing every eighth American, 1 in 5 households, 1 in 5 voters, and 1 in 2 viewers of prime time television. Older Americans also spend 2 in 5 consumer dollars and, in turn, almost 1 in 3 federal budget dollars is spent on their behalf. Our typical senior, Mrs. Perkins, is married and living with her husband, who is four years older. Unhappily, in three or four years she will be a widow and will be living alone.

The Perkinses live in a single-family detached home in one of eight states: California, New York, Florida, Pennsylvania, Texas, Illinois, Ohio, or Michigan. But there is a good chance they are considering a move to a sunbelt state. Both have 12 years of education. Mr. Perkins worked for 39 years.

The Perkinses retired at age 62 by choice and they receive $566 a month from Social Security. Their income is in the low 20 thousands. They own their own home, have a savings account, life insurance, and no debt. The couple is spending over half their budget on housing, food, and medical care and they worry that inflation will eat away at any leverage they have in their income. At the same time, they feel that they are better off financially than their parents were at their age.

The Perkinses have two children, grandchildren, and great-grandchildren. Family is a central theme in their lives. They see at least one child at least once a week and they help out their children by taking care of grandchildren. However, they insist that they do not want to live with their children or vice versa.

The Perkinses do work around their house including gardening and caring for their lawn. She says that she would like her husband to help more with the housework. He says that he would like more interesting meals and more frequent sex. They both have a driver's license and a car and they drive about 7,000 miles a year. They belong to the American Association of Retired Persons (AARP). They visit with friends three or more times a week and often help out others in need. They contribute to charity and devote time to their religion. The Perkinses also take a vacation every year, most often by car.

As do three in four of their peers, the Perkinses sometimes shop by mail. They are loyal to brand names, pay a little extra to save time and effort, and go out of their way to shop at stores that give good service. They both feel that advertisers are obsessed with youth. Out of the products and services that interest them the most, those relating to health care rank first.

While the Perkinses keep informed on world events and community issues, they feel alienated from the power structure. Along with four in five of their friends, they are against cuts in government spending for Social Security, Medicare and veterans' benefits and they favor a federal government program to provide long-term care to chronically ill and disabled seniors, adults, and children. At the same time they favor a cut in foreign aid.

The Perkinses report that they are happy with life, they like their age, and feel younger than their chronological years. Neither worries about death. In fact they say that they would trade two years of life for one year of good health.

The Perkinses view their health as excellent. She, however, has arthritis and her husband is showing signs of heart disease (from which he will die in a few years). The Perkinses do not smoke and drink only moderately. They are not overweight but they are perpetually dieting. They are more health conscious than they used to be, eating more fish and salads and avoiding fat.

This year the Perkinses will spend three days sick in bed and their activity will be restricted for another eight days due to illness. Each will visit a doctor nine times and each has a one in three chance of being hospitalized.

The Perkinses are Medicare beneficiaries. They pay an average of $5.50 per day out of their own pockets for health care and Medicare pays another $6.55 in their behalf. They also pay $1,200 annually for medical insurance to supplement Medicare. Understandably, on a recent survey the Perkinses answered that they worry that "health care costs will take a great portion of my assets."

Like virtually all of their contemporaries, both Mr. and Mrs. Perkins wear eyeglasses. Mrs. Perkins doesn't have osteoporosis, but one of every four women in her church's senior club does. Mr. Perkins has cataracts, as is true for one in five members of the church club. Incredibly, Mrs. Perkins and her husband are each taking six medications a day for assorted ailments.

The Perkinses do not presently need long-term care (services such as nursing home or home-health care for incapacitated individuals who require care for a long period of time). However, by her late 70s Mrs. Perkins will need help with daily activities such as shopping and getting around. She will receive that care at home as she prefers and a family member, most likely a daughter, will be the caregiver. Any "formal care" that she receives will be paid for out of her savings. In addition, sometime during their retirement Mrs. Perkins or her husband will be admitted to a nursing home from a hospital for at least a short time.

Mrs. Perkins will die at about age 84 from heart disease. Happily, however, when prior to her death Mrs. Perkins looks back on her senior years, she will find that they were significantly more secure and contented than her parents' were. The Perkinses had 14 years together after Mr. Perkins left the labor force compared to the 10 years that their parents had. They also had advantages that their parents did not have when they retired: improved Social Security benefits, Medicare, a pension, a vast network of programs and services for seniors, and a chipper view of age and aging that came into vogue in the 1970s and 1980s. Former president Ronald Reagan, who, at age 69, was the oldest president ever inaugurated, and 65-year-old first lady Barbara Bush, who is affectionately called the gray fox and admired for her grandmotherly ways, are indicative of this modern trend.

This is a portrait that the numbers in the *Fact Book on Aging* suggest. Obviously, it lacks the rich patina of individual experience, but as an abstract it is representative of every eighth American.

Fact Book
on Aging

Chapter 1

Aging America: Size and Growth of the Older Population

Senior Ranks Swell

A Thirtyfold Increase since 1870

Number of seniors in 1870: 1 million.[1]

In 1900: 3 million.[2]

In 1990: 31.6 million.[3]

Number of 55-plus persons in 1870: 2.8 million.[4]

In 1900: 7 million.[5]

In 1990: 53 million.[6]

Projections Show Growth Continuing

Projected number of seniors in 2000: 35 million.[7]

In 2030: 66 million.[8]

The rate of growth of seniors from 1990 to 2030: the senior population is expected to double.[9]

The projected number of 55-plus persons in 2000: 59 million.[10]

In 2030: 101 million.[11]

The rate of growth of 55-plus persons from 1990 to 2030: the 55 and over population is expected to more than double.[12]

Every Day in the United States

Every day in the United States: 6,000 Americans celebrate their 65th birthday.[13]

And: 3,800 Americans celebrate their 75th birthday.[14]

America's Seniors Outnumber All Canadians

The size of the American senior population compared to the entire population of Canada: the 65-plus American population is currently larger.[15]

The size of the American population over age 55 compared to the population of Canada: the 55-plus population is larger than twice the population of Canada.[16]

Senior Population Growth Outpaces All Other Age Groups

The portion of 65-plus people in the entire history of the world who are alive today: two-thirds.[17]

The rate of growth of seniors over the last two decades compared to the growth of the rest of the population: the senior population increased twice as fast.[18]

Since 1980, the average number of persons per month who have celebrated their 65th birthday: 168,000.[19]

Portion of Americans who will be eligible for Social Security and Medicare when the baby boom begins to retire early in the next century: 1 in 5 (compared to 1 in 8 today). [20]

Seniors Head More Households

The number of households headed by seniors in 1989: 20 million.[21]

Estimates for 2000: 22.6 million.[22]

America Ages

Median Age Advances

Median age of the population in 1820: 17 years.[23]

In 1900: 23 years.[24]

In 1990: 33 years.[25]

Number of years that were added to the median age from 1900 to 1970: 5 years.[26]

Years added since 1970: 5 years.[27]

Median age of the population projected in 2000: 36 years.[28]

In 2030: 42 years.[29]

Seniors Make Up a Larger Portion of Americans

Ratio of seniors in the population in 1900: 1 in 25.[30]

In 1990: 1 in 8.[31]

Projected ratio in 2030: 1 in 5.[32]

Ratio of 55-plus persons in the population in 1900: 1 in 10.[33]

In 1990: 1 in 5.[34]

The projected ratio in 2030: 1 in 3.[35]

Fewer Children, More Seniors

Percentage of children and teenagers in the population in 1900: 40 percent.[36]

Compared to percentage of seniors: 4 percent.[37]

Percentage of children and teenagers in 1990: 24 percent.[38]

Compared to percentage of seniors: 13 percent.[39]

Percentage of children and teenagers projected for 2030: 19 percent.[40]

Compared to percentage of seniors: 22 percent.[41]

Number of seniors versus children under age 14 for every square mile in the United States: 8 seniors versus 14 children.[42]

Fewer Workers per Senior

Number of seniors for every 100 persons of working age in 1900: 7.[43]

Number in 1990: 20.[44]

Projected number in 2030: 38.[45]

From Youngest-Old to Oldest-Old

The Youngest-Old

Portion of seniors who are age 65 to 74 (the youngest-old) in 1990: 6 in 10.[46]

Number of the youngest-old in 1990: 18.4 million.[47]

Projected portion of the youngest-old in the total population in 2030: 1 in 8—the same share of the population that the entire 65-plus population occupies today.[48]

The Middle-Old

Portion of seniors who are age 75 to 84 (the middle-old) in 1990: 3 in 10.[49]

Number of the middle-old in 1990: 9.9 million.[50]

The Oldest-Old

Portion of seniors who are 85-plus (the oldest-old) in 1990: 1 in 10.[51]

Number of the oldest-old in 1990: 3.3 million.[52]

The fastest-growing senior age group: the oldest-old.[53]

The size of the 85-plus population today compared to 1950: six times larger.[54]

Projected size of the 85-plus population in 2030 compared to 1990: at 8.1 million, 2 1/2 times larger.[55]

Alternative projections for 85-plus persons sponsored by the National Institute on Aging: 50 million in 2035 to 70 million in 2065.[56]

Americans Living Longer

Longevity of Persons Age 80 to 84

Portion of persons age 80 to 84 who were projected by the U.S. Census Bureau to live at least 5 years in 1986: 2 in 3.[57]

Projected for 2080: 3 in 4 persons this age are expected to live for at least 5 years.[58]

Passing the Century Mark

Growth in the number of Americans over 100 years old since 1950: the number of centenarians has grown more than 10 times.[59]

Estimates of the number of Americans over 100 years old: 25,000 to 46,000.[60]

The number of centenarians for every 10,000 seniors in the population: 9.[61]

When the first surviving members of the baby boom generation will reach 100: near the middle of the next century.[62]

The projected number of centenarians in 2080: 1 million.[63]

By 2080 the centenarian population is expected to increase by a factor of: 75.[64]

Black and White, Male and Female

White Seniors Outnumber Black Seniors

Percentage of whites who are over age 65 in 1990: 13 percent.[65]

Percentage of blacks who are over age 65: 8 percent.[66]

Percentage of seniors who are white: 90 percent.[67]

Percentage of seniors who are black: 8 percent.[68]

Number of white seniors: 28.3 million.[69]

Number of black seniors: 2.6 million.[70]

Black Senior Population Growing

Projected growth in the white senior population between 1990 and 2030: it is expected to double.[71]

Projected growth in the black senior population for this time period: it is expected to triple.[72]

The projected percentage of seniors in the white population in 2030: 23 percent.[73]

In the black population: 17 percent.[74]

The percentage of the older population that will be white in 2030: 83 percent.[75]

The percentage that will be black: 12 percent.[76]

Men in the Minority

Number of males versus females in the 65-plus age group in 1990: 13 million men and 19 million women.[77]

Ratio of 65-plus women compared to men: 3 to 2.[78]

Number of men per 100 women for the 65 to 69 age group: 83.[79]

For those 85-plus: 39.[80]

For centenarians: between 31 and 43.[81]

Senior Veterans

Veteran Population Patterns

Portion of 65-plus men who are veterans: 1 in 4.[82]

Portion who will be veterans in 2000: 2 in 3.[83]

By 2010: 1 in 2.[84]

By 2020: slightly over 1 in 3.[85]

Portion of veterans who are over age 65: 23 percent.[86]

Number of senior veterans projected for 2000: 9 million.[87]

For 2020: 7.7 million.[88]

The Oldest Veterans

The median age of veterans who served during World War II: 66.9 years.[89]

The median age for World War I vets: 91.6.[90]

Portion of senior veterans who are age 75 and over: 1 in 5.[91]

Portion who will be 75-plus in 2000: 2 in 5.[92]

In 2030: 3 in 5.[93]

Notes

1. U.S. Bureau of the Census, *Historical Statistics*, 1960: A 71–85.
2. U.S. Senate Special Committee on Aging, *Aging America*, 1987: 12.
3. U.S. Bureau of the Census, *Projections of the Population*, 1989: 42–43.
4. U.S. Bureau of the Census, *Historical Statistics*, 1960: A 71–85.
5. U.S. Senate Special Committee on Aging, *Aging America*, 1987: 12.
6. U.S. Bureau of the Census, *Projections of the Population*, 1989: 42–43.
7. U.S. Bureau of the Census, *Projections of the Population*, 1989: 63.
8. U.S. Bureau of the Census, *Projections of the Population*, 1989: 91.
9. There were 28.5 million seniors in 1985. The U.S. Census Bureau projects that there will be 59.2 million seniors in 2030 (middle-series projections). U.S. Bureau of the Census, *Projections of the Population*, 1989: 7.
10. U.S. Bureau of the Census, *Projections of the Population*, 1989: 63.
11. U.S. Bureau of the Census, *Projections of the Population*, 1989: 91.
12. There were 28.5 million seniors in 1985. The U.S. Census Bureau projects that there will be 59.2 million seniors in 2030 (middle-series projections). U.S. Bureau of the Census, *Projections of the Population*, 1989: 7.
13. Based on U.S. Bureau of the Census, *Projections of the Population*, 1989: 43.
14. Based on U.S. Bureau of the Census, *Projections of the Population*, 1989: 43.
15. The U.S. Bureau of the Census projects 31.6 million 65-plus Americans in 1990. U.S. Bureau of the Census, *Projections of the Population*, 1989: 43. The population of Canada was 25,334,000 in 1989. *World Almanac 1989*, 1988: 660.
16. The population of Canada was 25,334,000 in 1989. *World Almanac 1989*, 1988: 660.
17. Dychtwald, 1989: 6.
18. U.S. Senate Special Committee on Aging, *Aging America*, 1987: 1.
19. U.S. Senate Special Committee on Aging, *Aging America*, 1989: 1.
20. U.S. Senate Special Committee on Aging, *Aging America*, 1987: 9.
21. U.S. Bureau of the Census, *Households*, 1989: 5.
22. Exter, 1989: 75.
23. *World Almanac 1989*, 1988: 533.
24. *World Almanac 1989*, 1988: 533.
25. U.S. Bureau of the Census, *Projections of the Population*, 1989: 43.
26. U.S. Bureau of the Census, *Projections of the Population*, 1989: 4.
27. U.S. Bureau of the Census, *Projections of the Population*, 1989: 4.
28. U.S. Bureau of the Census, *Projections of the Population*, 1989: 63.
29. U.S. Bureau of the Census, *Projections of the Population*, 1989: 91.
30. U.S. Senate Special Committee on Aging, *Aging America*, 1987: 12.
31. U.S. Bureau of the Census, *Projections of the Population*, 1989: 42–43.
32. U.S. Bureau of the Census, *Projections of the Population*, 1989: 90–91.
33. U.S. Senate Special Committee on Aging, *Aging America*, 1987: 12.
34. U.S. Bureau of the Census, *Projections of the Population*, 1989: 42–43.
35. U.S. Bureau of the Census, *Projections of the Population*, 1989: 90–91.
36. Children and teenagers are under 17 years of age. U.S. Senate Special Committee on Aging, *Aging America*, 1989: 5.

37. U.S. Senate Special Committee on Aging, *Aging America*, 1989: 5.

38. U.S. Bureau of the Census, *Projections of the Population,* 1989: 42–43.

39. U.S. Bureau of the Census, *Projections of the Population,* 1989: 42–43.

40. U.S. Bureau of the Census, *Projections of the Population,* 1989: 90–91.

41. U.S. Bureau of the Census, *Projections of the Population,* 1989: 90–91.

42. Based on current population figures. U.S. Bureau of the Census, *Projections of the Population,* 1989: 43. *World Almanac 1989,* 1988: 408.

43. U.S. Senate Special Committee on Aging, *Aging America*, 1989: 11.

44. U.S. Senate Special Committee on Aging, *Aging America*, 1989: 11.

45. U.S. Senate Special Committee on Aging, *Aging America*, 1989: 11.

46. U.S. Bureau of the Census, *Projections of the Population,* 1989: 42–43.

47. U.S. Bureau of the Census, *Projections of the Population,* 1989: 42–43.

48. U.S. Bureau of the Census, *Projections of the Population,* 1989: 91.

49. U.S. Bureau of the Census, *Projections of the Population,* 1989: 42–43.

50. U.S. Bureau of the Census, *Projections of the Population,* 1989: 42–43.

51. U.S. Bureau of the Census, *Projections of the Population,* 1989: 42–43.

52. U.S. Bureau of the Census, *Projections of the Population,* 1989: 42–43.

53. U.S. Bureau of the Census, *Projections of the Population,* 1989: 42–42, 104–105.

54. U.S. Senate Special Committee on Aging, *Aging America*, 1987: 12. U.S. Bureau of the Census, *Projections of the Population,* 1989: 43.

55. U.S. Bureau of the Census, *Projections of the Population,* 1989: 91.

56. Otten, 1989: B1.

57. U.S. Bureau of the Census, *Projections of the Population,* 1989: 138.

58. U.S. Bureau of the Census, *Projections of the Population,* 1989: 138.

59. U.S. Bureau of the Census, *Centenarians,* 1987: 2.

60. U.S. Bureau of the Census, *Centenarians,* 1987: 1. U.S. Bureau of the Census, *Projections of the Population,* 1989: 9.

61. U.S. Bureau of the Census, *Centenarians,* 1987: 2.

62. U.S. Bureau of the Census, *Centenarians,* 1987: 1.

63. U.S. Bureau of the Census, *Centenarians,* 1987: 1.

64. U.S. Bureau of the Census, *Centenarians,* 1989: 2.

65. U.S. Bureau of the Census, *Projections of the Population,* 1989: 43.

66. U.S. Bureau of the Census, *Projections of the Population,* 1989: 43.

67. U.S. Bureau of the Census, *Projections of the Population,* 1989: 43.

68. U.S. Bureau of the Census, *Projections of the Population,* 1989: 43.

69. U.S. Bureau of the Census, *Projections of the Population,* 1989: 43.

70. U.S. Bureau of the Census, *Projections of the Population,* 1989: 43.

71. U.S. Bureau of the Census, *Projections of the Population,* 1989: 43, 91.

72. U.S. Bureau of the Census, *Projections of the Population,* 1989: 43, 91.

73. U.S. Bureau of the Census, *Projections of the Population,* 1989: 90–91.

74. U.S. Bureau of the Census, *Projections of the Population,* 1989: 90–91.

75. U.S. Bureau of the Census, *Projections of the Population,* 1989: 90–91.

76. U.S. Bureau of the Census, *Projections of the Population,* 1989: 90–91.

77. U.S. Bureau of the Census, *Projections of the Population,* 1989: 43.

78. U.S. Bureau of the Census, *Projections of the Population,* 1989: 43.

79. U.S. Senate Special Committee on Aging, *Aging America*, 1989: 10.

80. U.S. Senate Special Committee on Aging, *Aging America*, 1989: 10.

81. Based on 1980 data. U.S. Bureau of the Census, *Centenarians,* 1987: 5.

82. U.S. Senate Special Committee on Aging, *Aging America*, 1989: 17.

83. U.S. Senate Special Committee on Aging, *Aging America,* 1989: 17.
84. U.S. Senate Special Committee on Aging, *Aging America,* 1989: 17.
85. U.S. Senate Special Committee on Aging, *Aging America,* 1989: 17.
86. U.S. Senate Special Committee on Aging, *Aging America,* 1989: 17.
87. U.S. Senate Special Committee on Aging, *Aging America,* 1989: 17.
88. U.S. Senate Special Committee on Aging, *Aging America,* 1989: 17.
89. U.S. Senate Special Committee on Aging, *Aging America,* 1989: 17.
90. U.S. Senate Special Committee on Aging, *Aging America,* 1989: 17.
91. U.S. Senate Special Committee on Aging, *Aging America,* 1989: 17.
92. U.S. Senate Special Committee on Aging, *Aging America,* 1989: 17.
93. U.S. Senate Special Committee on Aging, *Aging America,* 1989: 17.

Chapter 2

Life Expectancy and Longevity

People Live Longer than Ever Before

Gains in Life Expectancy since Ancient Times

Life expectancy at birth in ancient Rome and Greece: 20 years.[1]

In medieval Europe: 30 years.[2]

In Massachusetts in 1850: 38 years.[3]

In the United States in 1900: 47 years.[4]

Current life expectancy in the United States: 75 years.[5]

The number of years life expectancy has advanced so far in this century: 28 years.[6]

Future Generations Will Live Even Longer

U.S. Census Bureau projections for life expectancy at birth in the year 2000 for men: 74 years.[7]

For women: 80 years.[8]

In 2030 for men: 75 years.[9]

For women: 82 years.[10]

In 2080 for men: 74 years.[11]

For women: 85 years.[12]

Alternative projections of life expectancy by the Rand Corporation for the year 2000: 92 to 96 years.[13]

Older American Population on the Rise

In the half decade between 1930 and 1980 the number of persons over age 65 gained for every 100 babies born: 23.[14]

The number of persons over 80 gained per 100 persons reaching retirement age: 20.[15]

Death Rates Decrease for Men And Women

Deaths expected per 1,000 senior males in 1959 to 1961: 35.[16]

Deaths expected in 1986: 25.[17]

Deaths expected per 1,000 senior females in 1959 to 1961: 25.[18]

Deaths expected in 1986: 14.[19]

Americans Are Not the Longest-Lived

Rank of the United States for life expectancy at birth: no higher than 14th for men and 10th for women in the world.[20]

Ahead of the United States, among others, are: Japan, Sweden, the Netherlands, Switzerland, Norway, Australia, Canada and France.[21]

Women, Whites Live Longer

The Male/Female Longevity Gap

The gap in female/male life expectancy in 1900: women lived an average of 2 years longer than men.[22]

The current gap in life expectancy: women live an average of 7 years longer than men.[23]

Current life expectancy at birth for females: 78.4 years.[24]

Current life expectancy at birth for males: 71.5 years.[25]

Advance in life expectancy from 1940 to 1980 for women: 13 years.[26]

For men: 11 years.[27]

Since 1979 the gap in life expectancy for females and males has been reduced by: nine-tenths of a year.[28]

Number of male babies per 1,000 born alive in 1986 expected to survive to age 65: 731.[29]

Number of female babies per 1,000 born alive in 1986 expected to survive to age 65: 846.[30]

The White/Nonwhite Longevity Gap

The gap in life expectancy at birth by race in 1900: whites lived an average of 4.6 years longer than nonwhites.[31]

The current gap has changed only slightly: whites live an average of 4.3 years longer than nonwhites.[32]

Current life expectancy at birth for whites and nonwhites: 76 years for whites and 71 years for nonwhites.[33]

Hierarchy of life expectancy by race and sex: white females live the longest, followed by nonwhite females, white males, then nonwhite males.[34]

Largest gain in life expectancy since 1970: nonwhite females with a 6-year increase.[35]

Current life expectancy at age 65 for whites: 17 years.[36]

For nonwhites: 16 years.[37]

Poor Life Expectancy for Men Living in Harlem

Percentage of males living in Harlem who survive to age 65 compared with males living in Bangladesh: 40 versus 55 percent.[38]

Seniors Looking Forward

Life Expectancy at 65

Current life expectancy for Americans turning 65: 17 years.[39]

For men turning 65: 15 years.[40]

For women: 19 years.[41]

Gain in life expectancy since 1900 for men turning 65: 3 years.[42]

Gain for women: 7 years.[43]

Projected life expectancy for 65-plus men in 2050: 18 years.[44]

For women: 23 years.[45]

Life Expectancy at 85

Current life expectancy at age 85: 6 years.[46]

Percent increase in life expectancy at age 85 since 1960: 24 percent.[47]

Projected increase in life expectancy at age 85 by 2040: 44 percent.[48]

The Odds of Making It to 100

The odds of living to be 100 for a baby born in 1879: 400 to 1.[49]

The odds of living to be 100 for a baby born in 1980: 87 to 1.[50]

The odds of living to be 105: 559 to 1.[51]

The odds of living to be 110: 4,762 to 1.[52]

Exceeding Expectations

In a recent survey the remaining number of years that physicians thought an average 75-year-old woman had to live: under 5.[53]

The actual number of years she can expect to live: 12 more, to age 87.[54]

Life Expectancy Trivia

Baseball Players and Right-Handed Persons Live Longer

The number of days per month that have been added to average life expectancy at birth in this century: 10 days per month.[55]

The world's oldest living person as of January 1, 1990: Carrie White, who turned 115 on November 18, 1989, and received a certificate from the *Guinness Book of World Records* certifying her age.[56]

The greatest authenticated age: 120 years, 237 days.[57]

Age at which the oldest documented American died (in 1928): 115.[58]

Males who live longer on average than other males: baseball players.[59]

Life expectancy by type of handedness: after age 33 left-handed individuals are 1 to 2 percent per year more likely to die than right-handers.[60]

Life span extension predicted by Benjamin Franklin in 1780: 1,000-plus years.[61]

The state or district with the highest life expectancy: Hawaii with 77 years.[62]

The state or district with the lowest life expectancy: the District of Columbia with 69 years.[63]

The top states for life expectancy in rank order: Hawaii, Iowa, North Dakota, Utah, Nebraska, Kansas, Colorado, Idaho, Minnesota, Washington, Connecticut and Massachusetts, all with over 75 years in life expectancy.[64]

Notes

1. Soldo, 1988: 6.
2. Soldo, 1988: 6.
3. U.S. Bureau of the Census, *Historical Statistics,* 1960: B 37–91.
4. U.S. Senate Special Committee on Aging, *Aging America,* 1987: 23.
5. The expectation of life at birth represents the average number of years that a group of infants would live if they were to experience throughout life the age-specific death rates prevailing in that year. Current life expectancy is for 1987, the latest year for which data are available. National Center for Health Statistics, *Advance Report of Final Mortality Statistics,* 1989: 14.
6. Life expectancy at birth was 47.3 years in 1900 and 75 years in 1987. U.S. Senate Special Committee on Aging, *Aging America,* 1989: 23. National Center for Health Statistics, *Advance Report of Final Mortality Statistics,* 1989: 14.
7. Middle mortality assumptions. U.S. Bureau of the Census, *Projections of the Population,* 1989: 153.
8. Middle mortality assumptions. U.S. Bureau of the Census, *Projections of the Population,* 1989: 153.

9. Middle mortality assumptions. U.S. Bureau of the Census, *Projections of the Population*, 1989: 153.

10. Middle mortality assumptions. U.S. Bureau of the Census, *Projections of the Population*, 1989 : 153.

11. Middle mortality assumptions. U.S. Bureau of the Census, *Projections of the Population*, 1989: 153.

12. Middle mortality assumptions. U.S. Bureau of the Census, *Projections of the Population*, 1989: 153.

13. Data are from the Rand Corporation. Reported in *Older Americans Reports*, November 21, 1989: 4.

14. U.S. Bureau of the Census, *Demographic and Socioeconomic Aspects of Aging*, 1984: 43.

15. U.S. Bureau of the Census, *Demographic and Socioeconomic Aspects of Aging*, 1984: 43.

16. U.S. Bureau of the Census, *Statistical Abstract 1989*, 1989: 72.

17. U.S. Bureau of the Census, *Statistical Abstract 1989*, 1989: 72.

18. U.S. Bureau of the Census, *Statistical Abstract 1989*, 1989: 72.

19. U.S. Bureau of the Census, *Statistical Abstract 1989*, 1989: 72.

20. National Center for Health Statistics, *Health: United States 1988*, 1989: 60.

21. National Center for Health Statistics, *Health: United States 1988*, 1989: 60.

22. U.S. Bureau of the Census, *Historical Statistics*, 1960: B 92–112.

23. Current life expectancy is for 1987, the latest year for which data are available. National Center for Health Statistics, *Advance Report of Final Mortality Statistics*, 1989: 1, 14.

24. Current life expectancy is for 1987, the latest year for which data are available. National Center for Health Statistics, *Advance Report of Final Mortality Statistics*, 1989: 1, 14.

25. Current life expectancy is for 1987, the latest year for which data are available. National Center for Health Statistics, *Advance Report of Final Mortality Statistics*, 1989: 1, 14.

26. National Center for Health Statistics, *Advance Report of Final Mortality Statistics*, 1989: 14.

27. National Center for Health Statistics, *Advance Report of Final Mortality Statistics*, 1989: 14.

28. National Center for Health Statistics, *Advance Report of Final Mortality Statistics*, 1989: 14.

29. U.S. Bureau of the Census, *Statistical Abstract 1989*, 1989: 72.

30. U.S. Bureau of the Census, *Statistical Abstract 1989*, 1989: 72.

31. U.S. Bureau of the Census, *Historical Statistics*, 1960: B 92–112.

32. Current life expectancy is for 1987, the latest year for which data are available. National Center for Health Statistics, *Advance Report of Final Mortality Statistics*, 1989 : 14.

33. Current life expectancy is for 1987, the latest year for which data are available. National Center for Health Statistics, *Advance Report of Final Mortality Statistics,* 1989: 14.

34. Based on life expectancy at birth for 1987, the latest year for which data are available. National Center for Health Statistics, *Advance Report of Final Mortality Statistics,* 1989: 14.

35. National Center for Health Statistics, *Advance Report of Final Mortality Statistics,* 1989: 14.

36. Current life expectancy is for 1987, the latest year for which data are available. U.S. Senate Special Committee on Aging, *Aging America,* 1989: 14.

37. Current life expectancy is for 1987, the latest year for which data are available. U.S. Senate Special Committee on Aging, *Aging America,* 1989: 14.

38. McCord, 1990: 173.

39. Current life expectancy figures are for 1987, the latest year for which data are available. U.S. Senate Special Committee on Aging, *Aging America,* 1989: 14.

40. Current life expectancy figures are for 1987, the latest year for which data are available. U.S. Senate Special Committee on Aging, *Aging America,* 1989: 14.

41. Current life expectancy figures are for 1987, the latest year for which data are available. U.S. Senate Special Committee on Aging, *Aging America,* 1989: 14.

42. Current life expectancy is for 1987, the latest year for which data are available. U.S. Senate Special Committee on Aging, *Aging America,* 1989: 14.

43. Current life expectancy is for 1987, the latest year for which data are available. U.S. Senate Special Committee on Aging, *Aging America,* 1989: 14.

44. U.S. Bureau of the Census middle mortality assumptions. U.S. Bureau of the Census, *Projections of the Population,* 1989: 153.

45. U.S. Bureau of the Census middle mortality assumptions. U.S. Bureau of the Census, *Projections of the Population,* 1989: 153.

46. Current life expectancy is for 1987, the latest year for which data are available. U.S. Bureau of the Census, *Statistical Abstract 1989,* 1989: 73.

47. Soldo, 1985: 227–247.

48. Soldo, 1985: 227–247.

49. U.S. Bureau of the Census, *Centenarians,* 1987: 2.

50. U.S. Bureau of the Census, *Centenarians,* 1987: 2.

51. U.S. Bureau of the Census, *Centenarians,* 1987: 2.

52. U.S. Bureau of the Census, *Centenarians,* 1987: 2.

53. University of California, August 1989: 1.

54. University of California, August 1989: 1.

55. Based on a gain in life expectancy of 28 years from 1900 to 1987.

56. *USA Today,* November 21, 1989: 2A.

57. Shigechiyo Izumi of Japan. *Guinness 1989,* 1988: 14. (Other sources report that he died at age 116.)

58. Vierck, 1988: 91.

59. Waterbor, 1988: 1278–1280.
60. Study by Dr. Stanley Coren at the University of British Columbia and Dr. Diane Halpern at California State University. Reported in *People,* November 6, 1989: 115.
61. Ettinger, 1964.
62. U.S. Bureau of the Census, *Statistical Abstract 1989,* 1989: 72.
63. U.S. Bureau of the Census, *Statistical Abstract 1989,* 1989: 72.
64. U.S. Bureau of the Census, *Statistical Abstract 1989,* 1989: 72.

Chapter 3

Geographic Distribution and Mobility

Where Seniors Live

Over Half of Seniors Live in Eight States

The eight states where over half of the senior population live: California, New York, Florida, Pennsylvania, Texas, Illinois, Ohio, and Michigan.[1]

State with the largest percentage of seniors: Florida with 18 percent.[2]

Followed by: Iowa, Pennsylvania, Rhode Island, Arkansas, and South Dakota, all with more than 14 percent.[3]

State with the smallest percentage of elderly persons: Alaska with 4 percent.[4]

Followed by: Utah, Wyoming, Colorado, and Texas, all with less than 10 percent.[5]

The state with the highest "retention expectation" (that portion of a person's lifetime that can be expected to be lived in the region of birth): Texas, where a newborn can expect to live 60 percent of his or her life in that state.[6]

By 2020 the state whose population over age 60 will be second only to Florida: Hawaii with 28 percent.[7]

More than 7 in 10 Hispanic seniors live in four states: California, Texas, Florida, and New York.[8]

Where the Oldest-Old Live

The state with the largest 85-plus population: California with 282,000.[9]

Followed by: New York with 235,000, and Florida, Pennsylvania, Illinois, and Ohio with between 100,000 and 180,000.[10]

The state with the smallest 85-plus population: Alaska with 1,000.[11]

Followed by: Wyoming, Delaware, Vermont, and Hawaii with 7,000 or fewer in each.[12]

State with the largest number of centenarians: California with 2,155 in 1980.[13]

The state with the smallest number of centenarians: Alaska with 9 in 1980.[14]

Oldest and Youngest State Populations

State with the highest median age: Florida with 36.3 years,[15] followed by Connecticut and New Jersey with 34.2 and Pennsylvania with 34.1.[16]

State with lowest median age: Utah, with 25.5 years,[17] followed by Alaska, Louisiana, Mississippi, Texas, and Wyoming with median ages of less than 30 years.[18]

Pulling Up Roots

From Here to There

Percentage of senior householders who moved between March 1985 and March 1986: 4.[19]

Areas where increase in the 65-plus population is most rapid: the South and West.[20]

The top five states where 65-plus persons move from: New York, California, Illinois, Florida, and New Jersey.[21]

The top five states where 65-plus persons move to: Florida, California, Arizona, Texas, and New Jersey.[22]

States with more than a 50-percent increase in their senior populations in the last decade: Alaska and Nevada.[23]

Senior Influx Means Dollars to Some States

Amount of money Florida will have gained from persons over age 60 who moved there from 1985 to 1990 to retire: $6 billion.[24]

States that will have gained $100 million or more from persons over age 60 retiring in them during the same period: Texas, North Carolina, Arkansas, Oregon, South Carolina, Nevada, Georgia, Washington, New Mexico, and California.[25]

Senior Exodus Means Loss for Other States

Amount of money New York will have lost from persons over age 60 moving away from 1985 to 1990: $2.9 billion.[26]

Amount of money New Yorkers alone retiring to Florida will have deposited in the Sunshine State's economy over the five-year period: $1.7 billion.[27]

Amount of money retirees from New York and Illinois will have deposited in California's economy: $100 million.[28]

City, Country, or Suburbs

The Graying of the Suburbs

The number of senior households in the suburbs in 1985: 7.5 million.[29]

The number in urban areas: 6.2 million.[30]

The increase from 1970 to 1980 in the number of seniors living in the suburbs: 70 percent.[31]

The only major metropolitan area with over a million elderly: New York City.[32]

Seniors as a percentage of the rural as opposed to the general population: 25 versus 12.[33]

Notes

1. U.S. Bureau of the Census, *State Population and Household Estimates,* 1988: 30–79.
2. U.S. Bureau of the Census, *State Population and Household Estimates,* 1988: 30–79.
3. U.S. Bureau of the Census, *State Population and Household Estimates,* 1988: 30–79.
4. U.S. Bureau of the Census, *State Population and Household Estimates,* 1988: 30.
5. U.S. Bureau of the Census, *State Population and Household Estimates,* 1988: 30–79.
6. National Institute on Aging, *Special Report,* 1988: 15.
7. Study by Andrei Rogers at the University of Colorado. Reported in National Institute on Aging, *Special Report,* 1988: 15.
8. National Council of La Raza, 1987: 1.
9. U.S. Bureau of the Census, *State Population and Household Estimates,* 1988: 30–79.
10. U.S. Bureau of the Census, *State Population and Household Estimates,* 1988: 30–79.
11. U.S. Bureau of the Census, *State Population and Household Estimates,* 1988: 30–79.
12. U.S. Bureau of the Census, *State Population and Household Estimates,* 1988: 30–79.
13. U.S. Bureau of the Census, *Centenarians,* 1987: B12.
14. U.S. Bureau of the Census, *Centenarians,* 1987: B6.
15. U.S. Bureau of the Census, *State Population and Household Estimates,* 1988: 30–79.
16. U.S. Bureau of the Census, *State Population and Household Estimates,* 1988: 30–79.
17. U.S. Bureau of the Census, *State Population and Household Estimates,* 1988: 30–79.
18. U.S. Bureau of the Census, *State Population and Household Estimates,* 1988: 30–79.
19. U.S. Department of Commerce, *American Housing Survey,* 1988: 288.
20. U.S. Senate Special Committee on Aging, *Aging America,* 1987: 34.
21. U.S. Senate Special Committee on Aging, *Aging America,* 1987: 34.
22. U.S. Senate Special Committee on Aging, *Aging America,* 1987: 34.
23. U.S. Senate Special Committee on Aging, *Aging America,* 1989: 18.
24. Longino, 1989: 28–31.
25. Longino, 1989: 28–31.
26. Longino, 1989: 28–31.
27. Longino, 1989: 28–31.
28. Longino, 1989: 28–31.
29. U.S. Department of Commerce, *American Housing Survey,* 1988: 10.
30. U.S. Department of Commerce, *American Housing Survey,* 1988: 10.
31. Transportation Research Board, 1988: 27.
32. U.S. Senate Special Committee on Aging, *Aging America,* 1987: 30.
33. U.S. Senate Special Committee on Aging, *Aging Reports,* 1989: 6.

Chapter 4

Work and Retirement

Seniors in the Work Force

Americans Spend More Time Working

Average number of years men worked in 1900: 32.[1]
In 1980: 39.[2]
Average number of years women worked in 1900: 6.[3]
In 1980: 29.[4]

Work Life Expectancy

Average remaining work life expectancy for males and females at age 60: 4 years for males and 3 years for females.[5]

Average remaining work life expectancy for males and females at age 65: 2 years for each.[6]

Workers over 50

Men age 50 to 54 who are in the labor force: 9 in 10.[7]

Men at age 60 to 64: slightly over half.[8]

Men at age 70 and older: 1 in 10.[9]

Women age 50 to 54 who are in the labor force: 7 in 10.[10]

Women at age 60 to 64: one-third.[11]

Women at age 70: 1 in 20.[12]

Seniors at Work

Portion of the labor force that is age 55 to 64: 10 percent.[13]

Portion that is 65-plus: 3 percent.[14]

Number of persons age 55 to 64 presently in the labor force: 12 million.[15]

Number of persons over age 65: 3 million.[16]

Percentage of persons age 65 and older who are in the labor force: 11.[17]

Percentage of men age 65 and older who are in the labor force: 17.[18]

Percentage of women age 65 and older who are in the labor force: 8.[19]

Percentage of 65-plus white females who work: 8.[20]

Percentage of 65-plus black females who work: 10.[21]

Percentage of 65-plus white men who work: 17.[22]

Percentage of older black men who work: 14.[23]

Older Women Are Working More

Increase in women's share of the 55-plus paid work force between 1950 and 1987: their share doubled.[24]

The reason why the share of women in the 55-plus work force doubled: because of the increasing trend of males retiring earlier.[25]

Future Seniors Will Work Less

The portion of 65-plus men expected to be working in 2000: 1 in 10.[26]

The portion of older women: 1 in 20.[27]

Percentage of the labor force that is expected to be age 65 and over in 2000: 2.[28]

Number of 55-plus men expected to be working in 2000: 8.6 million.[29]

Number of 55-plus women: 6.8 million.[30]

What Seniors Do

The occupations of three-quarters of workers 65 and over: managerial and professional; technical, sales, and administrative support; and service occupations.[31]

Percentage of adults over age 50 who say they have a strong need to start a new business or line of work: 16.[32]

What Seniors Earn

Median earnings of year-round full-time 65-plus workers in 1987: $19,418.[33]

Of men: $25,382.[34]

Of women: $15,200.[35]

How Employers View Older Workers

The percentage of executives of small businesses who oppose forcing people to retire at a certain age: 71.[36]

According to a recent study, the percentage of business managers who view older workers as having good attendance: 86.[37]

Percentage who think that they are committed to quality: 82.[38]

Percentage who think that they are loyal and dedicated: 79.[39]

Percentage who think they have practical knowledge: 76.[40]

Percentage who think they have solid experience: 74.[41]

Percentage who think they perform reliably: 71.[42]

Percentage who think they have the ability to get along with coworkers 60.[43]

Employers' Attitudes toward Strengthening the Role of Older Workers

Based on a 1989 survey of 400 company human resource executives by the American Association of Retired Persons (AARP):

Percentage of companies that have a formal program focused on utilizing workers who are 50 and over: 25.[44]

Portion of companies that have adopted measures such as skill training to fully use older workers: 3 in 10.[45]

Percentage of employers who view phased retirement as effective: 45.[46]

Percentage who actually have phased retirement programs: 18.[47]

Percentage of companies that had or were considering early retirement programs as a means to reduce costs: 61 percent of companies with 500 to 999 employees and 44 percent with 1,000 employees or more.[48]

Combining Work and Retirement

Portion of the labor force that would prefer to continue some kind of paid part-time work after retirement: about three-quarters.[49]

Portion of workers age 55 and over who feel that a job that allows one or two days per week at home after retirement would be beneficial: 74 percent.[50]

Portion who feel that a job shared with someone else would be beneficial: 71 percent.[51]

Number of able workers age 50 to 64 who are available for work: 1.1 million.[52]

Seniors Out of Work

The unemployment rate for persons age 65 and over: not quite 3 percent.[53]

Number of weeks of unemployment for workers aged 55 to 64 in 1987: 22 weeks compared to 11 weeks for workers age 20 to 24.[54]

The unemployment rate for men age 65 or older if discouraged workers are counted: 4.8 percent.[55] (Discouraged workers want a job but do not look for work because they think no jobs are available or that they would not be hired.)

The unemployment rate for women age 65 or older including discouraged workers: 7.1 percent.[56]

Retirement

Planning for Retirement

Percentage of persons 45 to 54 who are skeptical about the government's ability to maintain adequate resources for retirees by the year 2000: 40.[57]

Percentage of persons over age 65: 23.[58]

According to a study at Harvard University, the factor which has the greatest influence on the decision to retire: availability of private pension coverage.[59]

Leaving Work

Portion of retirees age 65 and over who report that they left the work force by choice: almost two-thirds.[60]

Of the one-third of older workers who report that they were forced to retire, the portion who report that they retired because of disability or poor health: close to two-thirds.[61]

Portion who report that they retired because their employers had a mandatory retirement age: 20 percent.[62]

Of those who retire for reasons other than health, the portion who are still able to perform work but say they choose not to: two-thirds.[63]

Americans Spend More Time in Retirement

Average number of years men spent in retirement or other activities outside the labor force in 1900: 1.2 years.[64]

Average in 1980: 13.6 years.[65]

Proportion of retirees who leave work before age 65: two-thirds.[66]

The median age of retirement: 60.6.[67]

Military Retiree Patterns

Number of retired military personnel in the United States: 1.4 million.[68]

Projected number by 2000: 1.7 million.[69]

Total annual retirement benefits of retired military personnel: $17.5 billion.[70]

Notes to Chapter 4

1. U.S. Senate Special Committee on Aging, *Aging America,* 1987: 81.
2. U.S. Senate Special Committee on Aging, *Aging America,* 1987: 81.
3. U.S. Senate Special Committee on Aging, *Aging America,* 1987: 81.
4. U.S. Senate Special Committee on Aging, *Aging America,* 1987: 81.

5. U.S. Senate Special Committee on Aging, *Aging America,*
   1989: 64.
6. U.S. Senate Special Committee on Aging, *Aging America,*
   1989: 64.
7. Data are for 1988. U.S. Department of Labor, *Employment and Earnings,* 1989:
   162–164.
8. Data are for 1988. U.S. Department of Labor, *Employment and Earnings,* 1989:
   162–164.
9. Data are for 1988. U.S. Department of Labor, *Employment and Earnings,* 1989:
   162–164.
10. Data are for 1988. U.S. Department of Labor, *Employment and Earnings,* 1989:
    162–164.
11. Data are for 1988. U.S. Department of Labor, *Employment and Earnings,* 1989:
    162–164.
12. Data are for 1988. U.S. Department of Labor, *Employment and Earnings,* 1989:
    162–164.
13. Data are for 1988. U.S. Department of Labor, *Employment and Earnings,* 1989:
    162–164.
14. Data are for 1988. U.S. Department of Labor, *Employment and Earnings,* 1989:
    162–164.
15. Data are for 1988. U.S. Department of Labor, *Employment and Earnings,* 1989:
    162–164.
16. Data are for 1988. U.S. Department of Labor, *Employment and Earnings,* 1989:
    162–164.
17. Data are for 1988. U.S. Department of Labor, *Employment and Earnings,* 1989:
    162–164.
18. Data are for 1988. U.S. Department of Labor, *Employment and Earnings,* 1989:
    162–164.
19. Data are for 1988. U.S. Department of Labor, *Employment and Earnings,* 1989:
    162–164.
20. Data are for 1988. U.S. Department of Labor, *Employment and Earnings,* 1989:
    162–164.
21. Data are for 1988. U.S. Department of Labor, *Employment and Earnings,* 1989:
    162–164.
22. Data are for 1988. U.S. Department of Labor, *Employment and Earnings,* 1989:
    162–164.
23. Data are for 1988. U.S. Department of Labor, *Employment and Earnings,* 1989:
    162–164.
24. U.S. Senate Special Committee on Aging, *Aging America,* 1989:
    72–73.
25. U.S. Senate Special Committee on Aging, *Aging America,* 1989:
    72–73.
26. Kutscher, 1988: 8.
27. Kutscher, 1988: 8.
28. Kutscher, 1988: 12.
29. Fullerton, 1987: 20.
30. Fullerton, 1987: 20.
31. U.S. Senate Special Committee on Aging, 1989: 71.
32. Daniel Yankelovich Group, 1987: 15.

33. U.S. Department of Labor, *Problems,* 1989: 38.
34. U.S. Department of Labor, *Problems,* 1989: 38.
35. U.S. Department of Labor, *Problems,* 1989: 38.
36. Reliable Corporation survey of 3,100 small business executives and owners. Reported in Parker, 1990: B1.
37. *Mature Market Report,* March 1988: 10.
38. *Mature Market Report,* March 1988: 10.
39. *Mature Market Report,* March 1988: 10.
40. *Mature Market Report,* March 1988: 10.
41. *Mature Market Report,* March 1988: 10.
42. *Mature Market Report,* March 1988: 10.
43. *Mature Market Report,* March 1988: 10.
44. Stephens, December 1989: 1.
45. Stephens, December 1989: 4.
46. Stephens, December 1989: 5.
47. Stephens, December 1989: 5.
48. Stephens, December 1989: 5.
49. Survey conducted by Lou Harris and Associates in 1981. Reported in U.S. Senate Special Committee on Aging, *Aging America,* 1989: 73.
50. Survey conducted by Lou Harris and Associates in 1981. Reported in U.S. Senate Special Committee on Aging, *Aging America,* 1989: 73.
51. Survey conducted by Lou Harris and Associates in 1981. Reported in U.S. Senate Special Committee on Aging, *Aging America,* 1989: 73.
52. Survey conducted by Lou Harris and Associates for the Commonwealth Fund. Reported in *Older Americans Reports,* January 26, 1990: 36.
53. Data are for 1988, the latest year for which data are available. U.S. Department of Labor, *Employment,* 1989: 162.
54. U.S. Senate Special Committee on Aging, *Aging America,* 1989: 75.
55. U.S. Department of Labor, *Problems,* 1989: 15.
56. U.S. Department of Labor, *Problems,* 1989: 15.
57. Survey conducted by New World Decisions. Reported in *Older Americans Reports,* February 24, 1989: 73.
58. Survey conducted by New World Decisions. Reported in *Older Americans Reports,* February 24, 1989: 73.
59. Study by David Wise at Harvard University. Reported in National Institute on Aging, *Special Report,* 1988: 32.
60. 1981 Survey by Lou Harris. Reported in U.S. Senate Special Committee on Aging, *Aging America,* 1987: 92.
61. 1981 Survey by Lou Harris. Reported in U.S. Senate Special Committee on Aging, *Aging America,* 1987: 92.
62. 1981 Survey by Lou Harris. Reported in U.S. Senate Special Committee on Aging, *Aging America,* 1987: 92.
63. Data are from the National Center for Health Statistics. Reported in *Older Americans Reports,* May 29, 1987: 8.
64. U.S. Senate Special Committee on Aging, *Aging America,* 1987: 81.

65. U.S. Senate Special Committee on Aging, *Aging America,*
    1987: 81.
66. U.S. Senate Special Committee on Aging, *Aging America,*
    1987: 84.
67. U.S. Senate Special Committee on Aging, *Aging America,*
    1987: 84.
68. *Mature Market Report,* December 1987: 9.
69. *Mature Market Report,* December 1987: 9.
70. *Mature Market Report,* December 1987: 9.

Chapter 5

Seniors and Money

Attitudes about Money

Money Worries

In a survey by the *Wall Street Journal,* the portion of retirees who say they aren't as comfortable financially as during their working years: more than half.[1]

The portion who say their standard of living is "a lot lower than before": nearly one-fifth.[2]

And in a large study by the Independent Sector, the percentage of persons age 65 to 74 who say that they worry about not having enough money in the future: 45.[3]

Percentage of those over age 75 who say they worry: 34.[4]

And in a study of 500 seniors for Transamerica Life Companies, the percentage of seniors who say that "inflation will eat away at a large part of my savings": 73.[5]

Lack of Knowledge about Personal Finances

Percentage of seniors who don't know the dollar value of their assets, including the equity in their homes: 68.[6]

Percentage who don't know how much income they will receive from Social Security when they retire: 39.[7]

Percentage who don't know how much they will receive from a company pension: 46.[8]

Percentage who don't know how much they will receive from other sources: 54.[9]

Seniors in Poverty

Senior Poverty Levels

Official poverty level for unrelated individuals (not living in a family) over age 65 in 1988: $5,674.[10]

For a two-person household with householder over age 65: $7,158.[11]

Oldest and Youngest Are the Poorest

Percentage of seniors with incomes below the poverty level in 1988: 12.[12]

In other words: 1 in 8 seniors is poor.[13]

Compared to the poverty rate for adults age 18 to 64: 1 in 10.[14]

Compared to the poverty rate for children under 18: 1 in 10.[15]

Seniors as a portion of all poor persons in the United States in 1988: more than 1 in 10 (11 percent).[16]

Children under 18 years and seniors as a portion of the nation's poor in 1988: half.[17]

Millions of Seniors Live in Poverty

Number of seniors living in poverty in 1988: 3,482,000.[18]

65-plus whites living in poverty: 2,595,000.[19]

65-plus blacks: 785,000.[20]

65-plus Hispanics: 225,000.[21]

The number of senior men: 965,000.[22]

Senior women: 2,518,000.[23]

Women, Blacks, and Hispanics Are Hardest Hit

Poverty rate for white persons over age 65 in 1988: 1 in 10.[24]

The rate for blacks over age 65: 1 in 3.[25]

The rate for Hispanics over age 65: 1 in 4.[26]

Older women and poverty in 1988: 3 in 4 poor seniors are women.[27]

The poverty rate for senior males: 1 in 12.[28]

The poverty rate for senior females: 1 in 7.[29]

Portion of older white women living in poverty in 1988: 1 in 8.[30]

Portion of black women: an astounding 2 in 5.[31]

Portion of Hispanic women: 1 in 4.[32]

Portion of white men: 1 in 15.[33]

Portion of black men: 1 in 4.[34]

Portion of Hispanic men: 1 in 6.[35]

Singles More Likely To Be Poor

Portion of senior married couple families living in poverty in 1988: 1 in 19.[36]

Portion of white senior married couples: 1 in 24.[37]

Portion of black senior married couples: 1 in 5.[38]

Portion of Hispanic senior married couples: 1 in 6.[39]

Portion of unrelated individuals (unrelated individuals are those not living with any relatives): 1 in 4.[40]

Portion of white unrelated individuals: 1 in 5.[41]

Portion of black unrelated individuals: 1 in 2.[42]

Portion of Hispanic unrelated individuals: 1 in 2.[43]

The Worst and Best Off

The highest poverty rate in the country in 1988 for seniors: black families with a female householder over age 65, no husband present, and with related children under 18 at an astounding 58 percent.[44]

The second highest poverty rate in the country in 1988 for seniors: black female unrelated individuals at 57 percent.[45]

The lowest poverty rate in the country in 1988 for seniors: white families with a householder over age 65 at 5 percent.[46]

Senior Poverty Levels Declined from 1966 to 1977

The poverty level of seniors in 1966: 28.5 percent.[47]

Reduction in the poverty level from 1966 to 1977: cut in half to

14.1 percent due in part to the success of Social Security and other benefit programs.[48]

Living on the Edge

Seniors in 1987 who lived near or below poverty (with income of less than 1.5 times the official poverty level): more than 1 in 4.[49]

Number of seniors in 1987 who lived near or below poverty: 7.8 million.[50]

Seniors as a portion of all "near poor": 1 in 5.[51]

Disparities

The age group for which poverty is most likely to be long-term: seniors.[52]

The percentage of seniors eligible for the "safety net" Supplemental Security Income program for the poor who do not receive it: 49.[53]

Income and Assets

How Much Seniors Have in Income

Median income in 1988 of families with heads who are over age 65: $21,705.[54]

Income of families with heads over age 65 compared to families with heads age 55 to 64: 62 cents for every dollar.[55]

Median income in 1988 of males over age 65: $12,471.[56]

Income of 65-plus males compared to males age 55 to 64: 55 cents for every dollar.[57]

Median income in 1988 of females over age 65: $7,103.[58]

Income of 65-plus women compared to 65-plus men: 57 cents for every dollar.[59]

Income of women over age 75 compared to men this age: 68 cents for every dollar.[60]

Seniors who had incomes below $15,000 in 1988: 3 in 4.[61]

Compared to persons age 45 to 54: 2 in 5.[62]

Where It Comes From

Percentage of income of aged units that comes from Social Security, Railroad Retirement, or disability: 42.[63] (In an aged unit all members are over 65. A unit may include unrelated individuals.)

Percentage from earnings: 11.[64]

Percentage from pensions: 17.[65]

Percentage from interest dividends: 27.[66]

Percentage from other sources: 3.[67]

Multiple Income Sources

Percentage of aged units receiving income from Social Security, Railroad Retirement, or disability: 95.[68]

Percentage with income from earnings: 17.[69]

Percentage with income from pensions: 41.[70]

Percentage with income from interest dividends: 71.[71]

Percentage with income from unemployment compensation, workers compensation, or veterans' payments: 6.[72]

Percentage with income from AFDC, SSI, and general assistance: 7.[73]

Percentage with income from child support and alimony: 3.[74]

Percentage with income from food stamps: 5.[75]

Percentage with income from housing assistance: 8.[76]

Percentage who participated in at least one major welfare assistance program during a 32-month period: 18.[77]

Savings and Investments

Percentage of seniors with savings accounts: 83.[78]

Percentage with corporate stocks and bonds: 31.[79]

Percentage with tax-deferred annuities: 18.[80]

Percentage with income-producing and other real estate assets: 32.[81]

Percentage of seniors who own life insurance policies: 71.[82]

Percentage who own life insurance with cash value: 55.[83]

Among senior households with life insurance, the average amount of coverage: $13,300.[84]

Percentage of seniors' income that comes from assets: 26 in 1986, up from 16 percent in 1963.[85]

Percentage of seniors who had some income from assets in 1984: 67.[86]

Non–Social Security Government Benefits

Percentage of poor senior households receiving Supplemental Security Income: 32.[87]

Percentage receiving Medicaid: 36.[88]

Percentage receiving food stamps: 29.[89]

Percentage living in federally subsidized housing: 17.[90]

Home Equity

Portion of seniors who have $20,000 to $50,000 of equity in their homes: about half.[91]

Percentage of persons 65 to 74 who have more than $50,000 in their homes: 40.[92]

Percentage of persons 75 and over: 35.[93]

Most Seniors Savers, Not Debtors

Percentage of seniors with no debt: 75.[94]

Percentage with credit card debt: 16.[95]

Percentage of seniors' net worth that is in savings and checking accounts: 30.[96]

Seniors' share of savings dollars: 80 percent.[97]

Seniors' share of bank dollars: 60 percent.[98]

Percentage of persons over 50 who say they want to pay more attention to saving money: 40.[99]

Percentage who express a commitment to using more credit/charge cards: 14.[100]

Percentage of persons over 50 who hold the following types of credit cards:

- Department store card: 57[101]
- VISA: 40[102]

- Master Card: 29[103]
- Telephone charge card: 27[104]
- American Express: 11[105]

Social Security and Other Benefits

Government Benefits Rescue Many from Poverty

The value of Social Security benefits to aged units with incomes under $5,000: 77 cents of every dollar of income comes from Social Security.[106]

The portion of aged units who receive 80 percent or more of their income from Social Security: 3 in 10.[107]

The portion of all seniors who would be in poverty without Social Security: half.[108]

The national poverty level would double without: Social Security, Medicare, Medicaid, welfare, food stamps, and other benefits.[109]

The number of people that Social Security benefits lifted out of poverty in 1986: 15.1 million.[110]

How Much Seniors Receive from Social Security

The average retiree's monthly Social Security check in 1990: $566.[111]

The average retired couple's monthly check: $966.[112]

The maximum monthly benefit for an individual retiring in 1990: $975.[113]

The earnings level at which the government deducts $1 from a worker's Social Security check for every $3 earned: $9,360 for seniors age 65 to 69 in 1990. (Retirees over 70 may earn any amount without a reduction.)[114]

Maximum Supplemental Security Income Benefits for Low-Income Persons

The maximum federal Supplemental Security Income monthly benefit in 1989 for an individual: $368.[115] (Individual states may add to this amount.)

The maximum benefit for a couple: $553.[116] (Individual states may add to this amount.)

The Social Security Tax

The Social Security tax paid by employees: 7.65 percent with an equal amount paid by employer.[117]

The Social Security tax paid by the self-employed: 15.3 percent.[118]

Fewer than Half Have Pensions

The percentage of full-time private workers over age 60 covered by pension plans: 47.[119]

The percentage of all seniors with pension coverage: 35.[120]

The percentage with a future benefit entitlement: 50.[121]

Senior Spending

How It Breaks Down—Age 65 to 74

Portion of annual expenditures persons age 65 to 74 spend on housing (including utilities), food, and medical care: over half.[122]

- Of this, the percentage spent on housing (shelter and furnishings): 20.[123]
- On utilities: 9.[124]
- On food: 16.[125]
- On health care: 9.[126]

Percentage of annual expenditures persons age 65 to 74 spend on clothing: 4.[127]

Percentage on transportation: 19.[128]

Percentage on pension and life insurance: 5.[129]

Percentage on entertainment: 4.[130]

Percentage on cash contributions: 6.[131]

Percentage on other: 6.[132]

How It Breaks Down—Age 75 and Over

Portion of annual expenditures persons 75 and over spend on housing (including utilities), food, and medical care: over two-thirds.[133]

- Of this, the percentage spent on housing (shelter and furnishings): 23.[134]
- On utilities: 12.[135]
- On food: 17.[136]
- On health care: 15.[137]

Percentage of annual expenditures persons 75 and over spend on clothing: 4.[138]

Percentage on transportation: 14.[139]

Percentage on pension and life insurance: 2.[140]

Percentage on entertainment: 3.[141]

Percentage on cash contributions: 6.[142]

Percentage on other: 6.[143]

Average Annual Expenditures of Consumers Age 65 to 74

Every day in the United States: seniors age 65 to 74 spend $68 for consumer goods and services.[144]

Total average annual expenditures for consumers age 65 to 74: $16,898.[145]

Average annual expenditures for persons age 65 to 74 for housing (including utilities), food and medical care: $9,299.[146]

- Expenditures for shelter and furnishings: $3,402.[147]
- Expenditures for utilities: $1,593.[148]
- Expenditures for food: $2,767.[149]
- Expenditures for health care: $1,537.[150]

Expenditures for persons age 65 to 74 for clothing: $710.[151]

Expenditures for transportation: $3,233.[152]

Expenditures for pension and life insurance: $857.[153]

Expenditures for entertainment: $686.[154]

Expenditures for cash contributions: $1,070.[155]

Expenditures for other: $1,042.[156]

Average Annual Expenditures of Consumers Age 75 and Over

Every day in the United States: seniors age 75 and over spend $32 for consumer goods and services.[157]

Total average annual expenditures for consumers age 75 and over: $11,746.[158]

Average annual expenditures for persons age 75 and over for housing (including utilities), food, and medical care: $7,812.[159]

- Expenditures for shelter and furnishings: $2,727.[160]
- Expenditures for utilities: $1,349.[161]
- Expenditures for food: $1,975.[162]
- Expenditures for health care: $1,761.[163]

Expenditures for persons age 75 and over for clothing: $416.[164]

Expenditures for transportation: $1,627.[165]

Expenditures for pension and life insurance: $262.[166]

Expenditures for entertainment: $299.[167]

Expenditures for cash contributions: $658.[168]

Expenditures for other: $671.[169]

Notes

1. Carlson, 1989: B1.
2. Carlson, 1989: B1.
3. Independent Sector, 1988: 46.
4. Independent Sector, 1988: 46.
5. Survey of 1,000 adults conducted by New World Decisions for Transamerica Life Companies. Transamerica Life Companies, 1988.
6. Survey of 1,000 adults conducted by New World Decisions for Transamerica Life Companies. Transamerica Life Companies, 1988.
7. Survey of 1,000 adults conducted by New World Decisions for Transamerica Life Companies. Transamerica Life Companies, 1988.
8. Survey of 1,000 adults conducted by New World Decisions for Transamerica Life Companies. Transamerica Life Companies, 1988.
9. Survey of 1,000 adults conducted by New World Decisions for Transamerica Life Companies. Transamerica Life Companies, 1988.
10. U.S. Bureau of the Census, *Money Income,* October 1989: 88.
11. U.S. Bureau of the Census, *Money Income,* October 1989: 88.

12. U.S. Bureau of the Census, *Money Income,* October 1989: 57.
13. U.S. Bureau of the Census, *Money Income,* October 1989: 57.
14. U.S. Bureau of the Census, *Money Income,* October 1989: 5.
15. U.S. Bureau of the Census, *Money Income,* October 1989: 5.
16. U.S. Bureau of the Census, *Money Income,* October 1989: 5.
17. U.S. Bureau of the Census, *Money Income,* October 1989: 5.
18. U.S. Bureau of the Census, *Money Income,* October 1989: 57.
19. U.S. Bureau of the Census, *Money Income,* October 1989: 60.
20. U.S. Bureau of the Census, *Money Income,* October 1989: 61.
21. U.S. Bureau of the Census, *Money Income,* October 1989: 61.
22. U.S. Bureau of the Census, *Money Income,* October 1989: 66.
23. U.S. Bureau of the Census, *Money Income,* October 1989: 66.
24. U.S. Bureau of the Census, *Money Income,* October 1989: 66.
25. U.S. Bureau of the Census, *Money Income,* October 1989: 66.
26. U.S. Bureau of the Census, *Money Income,* October 1989: 66.
27. U.S. Bureau of the Census, *Money Income,* October 1989: 66.
28. U.S. Bureau of the Census, *Money Income,* October 1989: 66.
29. U.S. Bureau of the Census, *Money Income,* October 1989: 66.
30. U.S. Bureau of the Census, *Money Income,* October 1989: 66.
31. U.S. Bureau of the Census, *Money Income,* October 1989: 66.
32. U.S. Bureau of the Census, *Money Income,* October 1989: 66.
33. U.S. Bureau of the Census, *Money Income,* October 1989: 66.
34. U.S. Bureau of the Census, *Money Income,* October 1989: 66.
35. U.S. Bureau of the Census, *Money Income,* October 1989: 66.
36. U.S. Bureau of the Census, *Money Income,* October 1989: 70.
37. U.S. Bureau of the Census, *Money Income,* October 1989: 70.
38. U.S. Bureau of the Census, *Money Income,* October 1989: 70.
39. U.S. Bureau of the Census, *Money Income,* October 1989: 70.
40. U.S. Bureau of the Census, *Money Income,* October 1989: 76.
41. U.S. Bureau of the Census, *Money Income,* October 1989: 76.
42. U.S. Bureau of the Census, *Money Income,* October 1989: 76.
43. U.S. Bureau of the Census, *Money Income,* October 1989: 76.
44. U.S. Bureau of the Census, *Money Income,* October 1989: 74.
45. U.S. Bureau of the Census, *Money Income,* October 1989: 76.
46. U.S. Bureau of the Census, *Money Income,* October 1989: 68.
47. U.S. Bureau of the Census, *Money Income,* October 1989: 60.
48. U.S. Bureau of the Census, *Money Income,* October 1989: 60.
49. U.S. Senate Special Committee on Aging, *Aging America,* 1989: 28.
50. U.S. Senate Special Committee on Aging, *Aging America,* 1989: 28.
51. U.S. Bureau of the Census, *Money Income, October 1989:* 5.
52. Duncan, 1984.
53. Study by ICF Inc. for the American Association of Retired Persons (AARP) and
    the Commonwealth Fund Commission on Elderly People Living Alone.
    Reported in *Older Americans Reports,* February 3, 1989: 45.
54. U.S. Bureau of the Census, *Money Income,* October 1989: 32.
55. U.S. Bureau of the Census, *Money Income,* October 1989: 32.
56. U.S. Bureau of the Census, *Money Income,* October 1989: 42.
57. U.S. Bureau of the Census, *Money Income,* October 1989: 42.
58. U.S. Bureau of the Census, *Money Income,* October 1989: 42.

59. U.S. Bureau of the Census, *Money Income,* October 1989: 42.

60. U.S. Bureau of the Census, *Money Income,* October 1989: 42–43.

61. U.S. Bureau of the Census, *Money Income,* October 1989: 51.

62. U.S. Bureau of the Census, *Money Income,* October 1989: 51.

63. In an aged unit all members are over age 65. It includes unrelated individuals. March 1988 Current Population Survey. U.S. House of Representatives, Committee on Ways and Means, 1989: 922.

64. U.S. House of Representatives, Committee on Ways and Means, 1989: 922.

65. U.S. House of Representatives, Committee on Ways and Means, 1989: 922.

66. U.S. House of Representatives, Committee on Ways and Means, 1989: 922.

67. Other sources include unemployment compensation, SSI, AFDC, general assistance, child support and alimony, food stamps, and housing assistance. U.S. House of Representatives, Committee on Ways and Means, 1989: 922.

68. In an aged unit all members are over age 65. Includes unrelated individuals. March 1988 Current Population Survey. U.S. House of Representatives, Committee on Ways and Means, 1989: 922.

69. U.S. House of Representatives, Committee on Ways and Means, 1989: 922.

70. U.S. House of Representatives, Committee on Ways and Means, 1989: 922.

71. U.S. House of Representatives, Committee on Ways and Means, 1989: 922.

72. U.S. House of Representatives, Committee on Ways and Means, 1989: 922.

73. U.S. House of Representatives, Committee on Ways and Means, 1989: 922.

74. U.S. House of Representatives, Committee on Ways and Means, 1989: 922.

75. U.S. House of Representatives, Committee on Ways and Means, 1989: 922.

76. U.S. House of Representatives, Committee on Ways and Means, 1989: 922.

77. Data from the 1984 Survey of Income and Program Participation. Reported in *Older Americans Reports,* May 5, 1989: 174.

78. Survey of 1,000 adults conducted by New World Decisions for Transamerica Life Companies. Transamerica Life Companies, 1988.

79. Survey of 1,000 adults conducted by New World Decisions for Transamerica Life Companies. Transamerica Life Companies, 1988.

80. Survey of 1,000 adults conducted by New World Decisions for Transamerica Life Companies. Transamerica Life Companies, 1988.

81. Survey of 1,000 adults conducted by New World Decisions for Transamerica Life Companies. Transamerica Life Companies, 1988.

82. American Council of Life Insurance, 1988: 38.

83. Survey of 1,000 adults conducted by New World Decisions for Transamerica Life Companies. Transamerica Life Companies, 1988.

84. American Council of Life Insurance, 1988: 38.

85. U.S. Senate Special Committee on Aging, *Developments in Aging 1988,* 1989: 84.

86. U.S. Senate Special Committee on Aging, *Developments in Aging 1988,* 1989: 84.

87. Villers Foundation, 1987: 40.

88. Villers Foundation, 1987: 42.

89. Villers Foundation, 1987: 43.

90. Villers Foundation, 1987: 44.

91. Data from the U.S. Census Bureau. Reported in *Mature Market Report,* August 1988: 4.

92. Data from the U.S. Census Bureau. Reported in *Mature Market Report,* August 1988: 4.

93. Data from the U.S. Census Bureau. Reported in *Mature Market Report*, August 1988: 4.
94. *Mature Market Report*, March 1988: 6.
95. *Mature Market Report*, March 1988: 6.
96. U.S. Senate Special Committee on Aging, *Aging America*, 1987:
97. *Mature Market Report*, September 1988: 5.
98. *Mature Market Report*, September 1988: 5.
99. Daniel Yankelovich Group, 1987: 18.
100. Daniel Yankelovich Group, 1987: 18.
101. Daniel Yankelovich Group, 1987: 18.
102. Daniel Yankelovich Group, 1987: 18.
103. Daniel Yankelovich Group, 1987: 18.
104. Daniel Yankelovich Group, 1987: 18.
105. Daniel Yankelovich Group, 1987: 18.
106. U.S. Senate Special Committee on Aging, *Aging America*, 1987: 60.
107. U.S. Senate Special Committee on Aging, *Aging America*, 1987: 60.
108. Study by the U.S. Census Bureau. Reported in *Older Americans Reports*, January 6, 1989: 1.
109. Study by the U.S. Census Bureau. Reported in *Older Americans Reports*, January 6, 1989: 1.
110. American Association of Retired Persons (AARP), September, October 1989: 8.
111. American Association of Retired Persons (AARP), September, October 1989: 8.
112. Social Security Administration.
113. Social Security Administration.
114. Social Security Administration.
115. *Older Americans Reports*, February 3, 1989.
116. *Older Americans Reports*, February 3, 1989.
117. Social Security Administration.
118. Social Security Administration.
119. Social Security Administration, 1989.
120. May, 1983 Current Population Survey. Tabulations from the Employee Benefit Research Institute.
121. May, 1983 Current Population Survey. Tabulations from the Employee Benefit Research Institute.
122. Data on consumption patterns are from the U.S. Bureau of Labor Statistics, *Consumer Expenditure Survey: Interview Survey*, 1986. Unpublished data supplied by the Bureau. Percentages are rounded, therefore totals may differ slightly from components. Reported in U.S. Senate Special Committee on Aging, *Aging America*, 1989: 57.
123. Reported in U.S. Senate Special Committee on Aging, *Aging America*, 1989: 57.
124. Reported in U.S. Senate Special Committee on Aging, *Aging America*, 1989: 57.
125. Reported in U.S. Senate Special Committee on Aging, *Aging America*, 1989: 57.
126. Reported in U.S. Senate Special Committee on Aging, *Aging America*, 1989: 57.
127. Data on consumption patterns are from the U.S. Bureau of Labor Statistics, Consumer Expenditure Survey: Interview Survey, 1986. Unpublished data supplied by the Bureau. Reported in U.S. Senate Special Committee on Aging, *Aging America*, 1989: 57.
128. Reported in U.S. Senate Special Committee on Aging, *Aging America*, 1989: 57.
129. Reported in U.S. Senate Special Committee on Aging, *Aging America*, 1989: 57.

130. Reported in U.S. Senate Special Committee on Aging, *Aging America*, 1989: 57.
131. Reported in U.S. Senate Special Committee on Aging, *Aging America*, 1989: 57.
132. Reported in U.S. Senate Special Committee on Aging, *Aging America*, 1989: 57.
133. Data on consumption patterns are from the U.S. Bureau of Labor Statistics, Consumer Expenditure Survey: Interview Survey, 1986. Unpublished data supplied by the Bureau. Percentages are rounded, therefore totals may differ slightly from components. Reported in U.S. Senate Special Committee on Aging, *Aging America*, 1989: 57.
134. Reported in U.S. Senate Special Committee on Aging, *Aging America*, 1989: 57.
135. Reported in U.S. Senate Special Committee on Aging, *Aging America*, 1989: 57.
136. Reported in U.S. Senate Special Committee on Aging, *Aging America*, 1989: 57.
137. Reported in U.S. Senate Special Committee on Aging, *Aging America*, 1989: 57.
138. Data on consumption patterns are from the U.S. Bureau of Labor Statistics, Consumer Expenditure Survey: Interview Survey, 1986. Unpublished data supplied by the Bureau. Percentages are rounded, therefore totals may differ slightly from components. Reported in U.S. Senate Special Committee on Aging, *Aging America*, 1989: 57.
139. Reported in U.S. Senate Special Committee on Aging, *Aging America*, 1989: 57.
140. Reported in U.S. Senate Special Committee on Aging, *Aging America*, 1989: 57.
141. Reported in U.S. Senate Special Committee on Aging, *Aging America*, 1989: 57.
142. Reported in U.S. Senate Special Committee on Aging, *Aging America*, 1989: 57.
143. Reported in U.S. Senate Special Committee on Aging, *Aging America*, 1989: 57.
144. Based on the 1986 Consumer Expenditure Survey. Reported in U.S. Senate Committee on Aging, *Aging America*, 1989: 57.
145. Consumer units differ from households in that households can include more than one consumer unit. Data on consumption patterns are from the U.S. Bureau of Labor Statistics, Consumer Expenditure Survey: Interview Survey, 1986. Unpublished data supplied by the Bureau. Percentages are rounded, therefore totals may differ slightly from components. Data are based on consumer units, which denote one or more unrelated persons living together who pool their income to make joint expenditure decisions; all members of a household who are related; or a person living alone or who lives with others but is financially independent. Reported in U.S. Senate Special Committee on Aging, *Aging America*, 1989: 57.
146. Reported in U.S. Senate Special Committee on Aging, *Aging America*, 1989: 57.
147. Reported in U.S. Senate Special Committee on Aging, *Aging America*, 1989: 57.
148. Reported in U.S. Senate Special Committee on Aging, *Aging America*, 1989: 57.
149. Reported in U.S. Senate Special Committee on Aging, *Aging America*, 1989: 57.
150. Reported in U.S. Senate Special Committee on Aging, *Aging America*, 1989: 57.
151. Data on consumption patterns are from the U.S. Bureau of Labor Statistics, Consumer Expenditure Survey: Interview Survey, 1986. Unpublished data supplied by the Bureau. Percentages are rounded, therefore totals may differ slightly from components. Data are based on consumer units, which denote one or more unrelated persons living together who pool their income to make joint expenditure decisions; all members of a household who are related; or a person living alone or who lives with others but is financially independent. Reported in U.S. Senate Special Committee on Aging, *Aging America*, 1989: 57.
152. Reported in U.S. Senate Special Committee on Aging, *Aging America*, 1989: 57.
153. Reported in U.S. Senate Special Committee on Aging, *Aging America*, 1989: 57.

154. Reported in U.S. Senate Special Committee on Aging, *Aging America,* 1989: 57.

155. Reported in U.S. Senate Special Committee on Aging, *Aging America,* 1989: 57.

156. Reported in U.S. Senate Special Committee on Aging, *Aging America,* 1989: 57.

157. Based on the 1986 Consumer Expenditure Survey. Reported in U.S. Senate Special Committee on Aging, *Aging America,* 1989: 57.

158. Data on consumption patterns are from the U.S. Bureau of Labor Statistics, Consumer Expenditure Survey: Interview Survey, 1986. Unpublished data supplied by the Bureau. Percentages are rounded, therefore totals may differ slightly from components. Data are based on consumer units, which denote one or more unrelated persons living together who pool their income to make joint expenditure decisions; all members of a household who are related; or a person living alone or who lives with others but is financially independent. Reported in U.S. Senate Special Committee on Aging, *Aging America,* 1989: 57.

159. Reported in U.S. Senate Special Committee on Aging, *Aging America,* 1989: 57.

160. Reported in U.S. Senate Special Committee on Aging, *Aging America,* 1989: 57.

161. Reported in U.S. Senate Special Committee on Aging, *Aging America,* 1989: 57.

162. Reported in U.S. Senate Special Committee on Aging, *Aging America,* 1989: 57.

163. Reported in U.S. Senate Special Committee on Aging, *Aging America,* 1989: 57.

164. Data on consumption patterns are from the U.S. Bureau of Labor Statistics, Consumer Expenditure Survey: Interview Survey, 1986. Unpublished data supplied by the Bureau. Percentages are rounded, therefore totals may differ slightly from components. Reported in U.S. Senate Special Committee on Aging, *Aging America,* 1989: 57.

165. Reported in U.S. Senate Special Committee on Aging, *Aging America,* 1989: 57.

166. Reported in U.S. Senate Special Committee on Aging, *Aging America,* 1989: 57.

167. Reported in U.S. Senate Special Committee on Aging, *Aging America,* 1989: 57.

168. Reported in U.S. Senate Special Committee on Aging, *Aging America,* 1989: 57.

169. Reported in U.S. Senate Special Committee on Aging, *Aging America,* 1989: 57.

Chapter 6

Marital Status, Living Arrangements, and Family

Marriage, Widowhood, and Divorce

More Men Are Married

Percentage of men age 65 to 74 who are married and living with a spouse: 80.[1]

Percentage of women this age: 52.[2]

Percentage of men 75 and over: 67.[3]

Percentage of women this age: 24.[4]

Proportion of female centenarians who are married: less than one-tenth.[5]

Proportion of male centenarians: 2 to 3 in 10.[6]

Difference in age between husband and wife in the average senior household: the husband is 4.1 years older.[7]

Seniors Getting Married

Remarriage rates for older men as compared to older women: 7 times greater.[8]

The number of seniors who married in 1984: 70,000.[9]

Increase in senior brides from 1970 to 1984: 28 percent.[10]

Increase in brides 75 and over: 80 percent.[11]

The percentage of senior brides who marry older men: 58.[12]

The percentage who marry younger men: 34.[13]

The percentage of senior grooms who marry younger women: 86.[14]

The percentage who marry older women: 10.[15]

Widows Outnumber Widowers

Percentage of men age 65 to 74 who are widowed: 9.[16]

Percentage of women this age: 36.[17]

Percentage of men 75 and over: 24.[18]

Percentage of women this age: 66.[19]

The average age of widows: 56.[20]

The average age at which widows remarry: 53.[21]

The average age at which widowers remarry: 61.[22]

Average length of time widowers wait before remarrying: 3.7 years.[23]

Senior Divorce Rates Low

Percentage of men age 65 to 74 who are divorced: 5.[24]

Percentage of women this age: 6.[25]

Percentage of men 75 and over: 2.[26]

Percentage of women this age: 3.[27]

Number of displaced homemakers over age 55 (displaced homemakers are women whose principal job was homemaking and who lost their main source of income usually through divorce, but also through the death of a spouse): 8 million.[28]

Number of displaced homemakers over age 65 in 1987 : 6.2 million.[29]

Few Never Married

Percentage of men age 65 to 74 who never married: 5.[30]

Percentage of women this age: 5.[31]

Percentage of men 75 and over: 4.[32]

Percentage of women this age: 6.[33]

2 in 5 Persons Age 65 to 69 Will Be Widowed or Divorced

Percentage of women who are now 30 to 34 who are expected to be divorced by ages 65 to 69: 22.[34]

Percentage who are expected to be widowed: 20.[35]

Living Arrangements

Most Seniors Live in Families

Percentage of all seniors living in a family setting: 67.[36]

Percentage of men: 82.[37]

Percentage of women: 57.[38]

Percentage of older men living alone: 16.[39]

Percentage of older women: 41.[40]

Percentage of unmarried couples who are over age 65: 5.[41]

Number of unmarried couples over age 65: 118,000 in 1988.[42]

Portion of seniors living alone who are women: 4 in 5.[43]

Portion of centenarians who do not live in nursing homes, but by themselves, with family or friends: 45 to 55 percent.[44]

Living Arrangements of Widows Vary by Race

Percentage of white widows over age 65 who live with others: 30.[45]

Percentage of black widows: 46.[46]

Percentage of Hispanic widows: 56.[47]

Percentage of white widows over age 65 who live alone: 71.[48]

Percentage of black widows: 53[49]

Percentage of Hispanic widows: 45.[50]

More Seniors Living Alone

Seniors living alone in 1960 compared to 1984: one-fifth versus one-third.[51]

Percentage of seniors living with their spouses who also shared housing with other people in 1960 compared to 1984: 29 versus 16.[52]

Percentage of seniors residing with their adult children in 1960 compared to 1984: 40 versus about 22.[53]

Seniors, Their Descendants, and Their Siblings

More Generations

Average number of generations in a family alive simultaneously early in this century: 2 to 3.[54]

Average number today: 3 to 4.[55]

Average number expected by 2000: 4.[56]

The number of living parents versus the number of children for the average American 40-year-old married couple: 2.6 parents versus 2.2 children.[57]

Percentage of Americans over the age of 45 who are grandparents: 69.[58]

Portion of Americans over the age of 65 who are great-grandparents: half.[59]

Percentage of children who have more than four living grandparents and step-grandparents: 8.[60]

Percentage of senior households with children present: 4.[61]

The number of seniors in the American population per number of children under the age of 14: 3 seniors for every 5 children.[62]

The number of teenagers per number of seniors: 4 teenagers for every 5 seniors.[63]

Seniors and Their Children

Seniors with at least 1 living child: 4 in 5.[64]

Percentage of seniors with no living children: 19.[65]

Percentage with 1 living child: 18.[66]

Percentage with 2 living children: 25.[67]

Percentage with 3 living children: 16.[68]

Percentage with 4 or more living children: 23.[69]

Percentage of seniors who say they do or will live in proximity of their children: 48.[70]

Percentage of seniors who have a child who could reach them in less than 30 minutes: over half.[71]

Percentage who live more than an hour away: 13.[72]

Percentage of parents who are in daily contact with their children: 41.[73]

Percentage in contact at least once a week: 20.[74]

Percentage who see their children less than monthly: 6.[75]

Percentage of Americans who think it is a bad idea for older people to share a home with grown children: 45.[76]

Percentage of adults over 50 who say they have a strong need to spend time with their children: 49.[77]

Percentage of seniors who provide children or grandchildren with money: 45.[78]

Percentage who help out their children by taking care of grandchildren: 54.[79]

Seniors and Their Grandchildren

Percentage of Americans over the age of 45 who are grandparents: 69.[80]

Percentage over 50: 76.[81]

Americans over the age of 65 who are great-grandparents: half.[82]

Percentage of children who have more than four living grandparents and step-grandparents: 8.[83]

Percentage of seniors who say they have a strong need to spend time with their grandchildren: 58.[84]

Percentage of all child care arrangements provided by grandparents for employed mothers: 7.[85]

Number of grandparents providing child care for working mothers: 1.9 million.[86]

Seniors and Their Siblings

Percentage of seniors with no living siblings: 21.[87]

Percentage with one living sibling: 21.[88]

Percentage with two living siblings: 19.[89]

Percentage with three living siblings: 14.[90]

Percentage with four or more living siblings: 25.[91]

Notes

1. U.S. Bureau of the Census, *Marital Status and Living Arrangements, 1988,* 1989: 3.
2. U.S. Bureau of the Census, *Marital Status and Living Arrangements, 1988,* 1989: 3.
3. U.S. Bureau of the Census, *Marital Status and Living Arrangements, 1988,* 1989: 3.
4. U.S. Bureau of the Census, *Marital Status and Living Arrangements, 1988,* 1989: 3.
5. Based on 1980 data. U.S. Bureau of the Census, *Centenarians,* 1987: 7.
6. Based on 1980 data. U.S. Bureau of the Census, *Centenarians,* 1987: 7.
7. U.S. Department of Health and Human Services, *Databook on the Elderly,* 1987: 11.
8. U.S. Department of Health and Human Services, *Databook on the Elderly,* 1987: 11.
9. National Center for Health Statistics, *Health Statistics on Older Persons,* 1987: 25.
10. National Center for Health Statistics, *Health Statistics on Older Persons,* 1987: 25.
11. National Center for Health Statistics, *Health Statistics on Older Persons,* 1987: 26.
12. U.S. Bureau of the Census, *Statistical Abstract 1989,* 1989: 87.
13. U.S. Bureau of the Census, *Statistical Abstract 1989,* 1989: 87.
14. U.S. Bureau of the Census, *Statistical Abstract 1989,* 1989: 87.
15. U.S. Bureau of the Census, *Statistical Abstract 1989,* 1989: 87.
16. U.S. Bureau of the Census, *Marital Status and Living Arrangements, 1988,* 1989: 3.
17. U.S. Bureau of the Census, *Marital Status and Living Arrangements, 1988,* 1989: 3.
18. U.S. Bureau of the Census, *Marital Status and Living Arrangements, 1988,* 1989: 3.
19. U.S. Bureau of the Census, *Marital Status and Living Arrangements, 1988,* 1989: 3.
20. National Institute on Aging, *The Aging Woman,* undated: 25.
21. *New Choices,* May 1989: 13.
22. *New Choices,* May 1989: 13.
23. *New Choices,* May 1989: 13.
24. U.S. Bureau of the Census, *Marital Status and Living Arrangements, 1988,* 1989: 3.
25. U.S. Bureau of the Census, *Marital Status and Living Arrangements, 1988,* 1989: 3.
26. U.S. Bureau of the Census, *Marital Status and Living Arrangements, 1988,* 1989: 3.
27. U.S. Bureau of the Census, *Marital Status and Living Arrangements, 1988,* 1989: 3.
28. Displaced Homemakers Network, 1987: A1.
29. Displaced Homemakers Network, 1987: A1.

30. U.S. Bureau of the Census, *Marital Status and Living Arrangements, 1988,* 1989: 3.
31. U.S. Bureau of the Census, *Marital Status and Living Arrangements, 1988,* 1989: 3.
32. U.S. Bureau of the Census, *Marital Status and Living Arrangements, 1988,* 1989: 3.
33. U.S. Bureau of the Census, *Marital Status and Living Arrangements, 1988,* 1989: 3.
34. Study of census data by Peter Uhlenberg. Reported in Karen S. Peterson, December 27, 1989: 1D.
35. Study of census data by Peter Uhlenberg. Reported in Karen S. Peterson, December 27, 1989: 1D.
36. U.S. Bureau of the Census, *Marital Status and Living Arrangements, 1988,* 1989: 9.
37. U.S. Bureau of the Census, *Marital Status and Living Arrangements, 1988,* 1989: 9.
38. U.S. Bureau of the Census, *Marital Status and Living Arrangements, 1988,* 1989: 9.
39. U.S. Senate Special Committee on Aging, *Aging America,* 1989: 110.
40. U.S. Senate Special Committee on Aging, *Aging America,* 1989: 110.
41. U.S. Bureau of the Census, *Marital Status and Living Arrangements, 1988,* 1989: 64.
42. U.S. Bureau of the Census, *Marital Status and Living Arrangements, 1988,* 1989: 64.
43. U.S. Senate Special Committee on Aging, *Aging America,* 1989: 110.
44. Based on 1980 data. U.S. Bureau of the Census, *Centenarians,* 1988: 13–14.
45. U.S. Senate Special Committee on Aging, *Aging America,* 1989: 111.
46. U.S. Senate Special Committee on Aging, *Aging America,* 1989: 111.
47. U.S. Senate Special Committee on Aging, *Aging America,* 1989: 111.
48. U.S. Senate Special Committee on Aging, *Aging America,* 1989: 111.
49. U.S. Senate Special Committee on Aging, *Aging America,* 1989: 111.
50. U.S. Senate Special Committee on Aging, *Aging America,* 1989: 111.
51. Data are from the Congressional Budget Office. Reported in *Older Americans Reports,* April 29, 1988: 172.
52. Data are from the Congressional Budget Office. Reported in *Older Americans Reports,* April 29, 1988: 172.
53. Data are from the Congressional Budget Office. Reported in *Older Americans Reports,* April 29, 1988: 172.
54. U.S. Bureau of the Census, *Demographic and Socioeconomic Aspects of Aging,* 1984: 90.
55. U.S. Bureau of the Census, *Demographic and Socioeconomic Aspects of Aging,* 1984: 90.
56. U.S. Bureau of the Census, *Demographic and Socioeconomic Aspects of Aging,* 1984: 90.
57. *Atlantic Monthly,* September 1989: 16
58. *Atlantic Monthly,* September 1989: 16.
59. *Atlantic Monthly,* September 1989: 16.
60. *Atlantic Monthly,* September 1989: 16.
61. U.S. Department of Commerce, *American Housing Survey,* 1988: 304.

62. U.S. Bureau of the Census, *Projections of the Population,* 1989: 42–43.
63. U.S. Bureau of the Census, *Projections of the Population,* 1989: 42–43.
64. U.S. Bureau of the Census, *Statistical Abstract 1988,* 1987: 37.
65. U.S. Bureau of the Census, *Statistical Abstract 1988,* 1987: 37.
66. U.S. Bureau of the Census, *Statistical Abstract 1988,* 1987: 37.
67. U.S. Bureau of the Census, *Statistical Abstract 1988,* 1987: 37.
68. U.S. Bureau of the Census, *Statistical Abstract 1988,* 1987: 37.
69. U.S. Bureau of the Census, *Statistical Abstract 1988,* 1987: 37.
70. Transamerica Life Companies, 1988: 7.
71. American Association of Retired Persons (AARP), *Changing Needs,* undated: 48–49.
72. American Association of Retired Persons (AARP), *Changing Needs,* undated: 48–49.
73. American Association of Retired Persons (AARP), *Changing Needs,* undated: 48–49.
74. American Association of Retired Persons (AARP), *Changing Needs,* undated: 48–49.
75. American Association of Retired Persons (AARP), *Changing Needs,* undated: 48–49.
76. Weiss, *100%,* 1988. (not paginated)
77. Daniel Yankelovich Group, 1987: 17.
78. Harris, 1975: 74.
79. Harris, 1975: 74.
80. *Atlantic Monthly,* September 1989: 16.
81. Daniel Yankelovich Group, 1987: 21.
82. *Atlantic Monthly,* September 1989: 16.
83. *Atlantic Monthly,* September 1989: 16.
84. Daniel Yankelovich Group, 1987: 17.
85. U.S. Bureau of the Census, *Statistical Abstract 1989,* 1989: 370.
86. U.S. Bureau of the Census, *Statistical Abstract 1989,* 1989: 370.
87. U.S. Bureau of the Census, *Statistical Abstract 1988,* 1987: 37.
88. U.S. Bureau of the Census, *Statistical Abstract 1988,* 1987: 37.
89. U.S. Bureau of the Census, *Statistical Abstract 1988,* 1987: 37.
90. U.S. Bureau of the Census, *Statistical Abstract 1988,* 1987: 37.
91. U.S. Bureau of the Census, *Statistical Abstract 1988,* 1987: 37.

Chapter 7

Education and Native Language

Educational Level

Education Levels Increasing

The median level of education in 1900: 8 years.[1]

The median level of education in the 1980s: 12 years.[2]

Increase in the median level of education among seniors between 1970 and 1987: from 8.7 to 12 years.[3]

The median number of school years projected for persons 65 and over in 2000 compared to projections for persons 25 years and over: 12.4 years versus 12.8 years.[4]

Younger People Have More Education

Percentage of persons age 60 to 64 who are high school graduates compared to those age 25 and over: 67 versus 76.[5]

Percentage of persons over age 75 who are high school graduates: 42.[6]

Percentage of persons age 60 to 64 who have completed 4 or more years of college: 15.[7]

Percentage of those 75 and older: 9.[8]

Percentage of seniors with a doctorate: less than 1.[9]

Education Levels by Sex

Percentage of men age 60 to 64 who have completed high school: 64.[10]

Percentage of women: 69.[11]

Percentage of men age 60 to 64 who have completed college: 10.[12]

Percentage of women: 6.[13]

Education Levels by Race

The median years of school completed for white persons age 60 to 64: 12.5 years.[14]

For blacks: 10.7 years.[15]

For Hispanics: 8.6 years.[16]

Education Levels by State and Region

The median number of school years completed for Westerners 65 and over versus Southerners of the same age: 12.3 years compared with 11.4 years.[17]

Percentage of Westerners 65 and over who are high school graduates compared with Southerners: 62 versus 47.[18]

Among the 15 most populous states, the one with the highest portion of 65 and over high school graduates: Michigan with 65 percent.[19]

The state with the lowest portion: Missouri with 40 percent.[20]

Among the 15 largest metropolitan areas the locality with the highest portion of 65 and over high school graduates: the Washington, D.C./Maryland/Virginia area with 69 percent.[21]

The area with the lowest portion: Baltimore, Maryland, with 41 percent.[22]

Seniors Still Learning

The number of persons age 55 or older enrolled in high school or college courses in October of 1986: 159,000.[23]

The number who were age 55 to 64: 124,000.[24]

The number who were age 65 or older: 35,000.[25]

The number of persons age 55 and over who had taken adult education courses in 1984: 2.7 million.[26]

The number of persons 65 and over: 900,000.[27]

Growth in the number of seniors participating in adult education courses: 30 percent per year.[28]

The number of colleges that now permit elderly people to take classes for credit or audit: almost 1,000.[29]

Percentage of adults over age 50 who say they give a high priority to continuing education, such as courses or lectures: 30.[30]

Native Language

1 in 10 Seniors Speak a Foreign Language at Home

Percentage of persons age 65 to 74 who speak a language other than English at home: 9.[31]

Percentage of persons over age 75: 13.[32]

The most frequent foreign languages (in order): Spanish, Italian, German, Polish, French, and Yiddish.[33]

Notes

1. U.S. Senate Special Committee on Aging, *Aging America*, 1987: 81.
2. U.S. Senate Special Committee on Aging, *Aging America*, 1989: 111.
3. U.S. Senate Special Committee on Aging, *Aging America*, 1989: 111.
4. U.S. Bureau of the Census, *Demographic and Socioeconomic Aspects of Aging*, 1984: 99.
5. U.S. Senate Special Committee on Aging, *Aging America*, 1989: 113.
6. U.S. Senate Special Committee on Aging, *Aging America*, 1989: 113.
7. U.S. Senate Special Committee on Aging, *Aging America*, 1989: 113.
8. U.S. Senate Special Committee on Aging, *Aging America*, 1989: 113.
9. U.S. Bureau of the Census, *Statistical Abstract 1989*, 1989: 133.
10. U.S. Senate Special Committee on Aging, *Aging America*, 1989: 113.
11. U.S. Senate Special Committee on Aging, *Aging America*, 1989: 113.
12. U.S. Senate Special Committee on Aging, *Aging America*, 1989: 113.
13. U.S. Senate Special Committee on Aging, *Aging America*, 1989: 113.
14. U.S. Senate Special Committee on Aging, *Aging America*, 1989: 113.
15. U.S. Senate Special Committee on Aging, *Aging America*, 1989: 113.
16. U.S. Senate Special Committee on Aging, *Aging America*, 1989: 113.
17. U.S. Bureau of the Census, *Educational Attainment*, 1988: 49–52.
18. U.S. Bureau of the Census, *Educational Attainment*, 1988: 49–52.
19. U.S. Bureau of the Census, *Educational Attainment*, 1988: 53–55.
20. U.S. Bureau of the Census, *Educational Attainment*, 1988: 53–55.

21. U.S. Bureau of the Census, *Educational Attainment,* 1988: 56–58.
22. U.S. Bureau of the Census, *Educational Attainment,* 1988: 56–58.
23. U.S. Senate Special Committee on Aging, *Aging America,* 1989: 115.
24. U.S. Senate Special Committee on Aging, *Aging America,* 1989: 115.
25. U.S. Senate Special Committee on Aging, *Aging America,* 1989: 115.
26. U.S. Department of Education, Office of Educational Research and Improvement, "Participation in Adult Education, May 1984," (October 1986). Reported in U.S. Senate Special Committee on Aging, *Aging America,* 1987: 143.
27. U.S. Department of Education, Office of Educational Research and Improvement, "Participation in Adult Education, May 1984," (October 1986). Reported in U.S. Senate Special Committee on Aging, *Aging America,* 1987: 143.
28. Moody, 1988: 192
29. *Mature Market Report,* May 1988: 10.
30. Daniel Yankelovich Group, 1987: 15.
31. Based on the 1979 Bureau of the Census Ancestry and Language Survey. Reported in U.S. Department of Health and Human Services, *Databook on the Elderly,* 1987: 8.
32. Based on the 1979 Bureau of the Census Ancestry and Language Survey. Reported in U.S. Department of Health and Human Services, *Databook on the Elderly,* 1987: 8.
33. Based on the 1979 Bureau of the Census Ancestry and Language Survey. Reported in U.S. Department of Health and Human Services, *Databook on the Elderly,* 1987: 8.

Chapter 8

Housing

Senior Households

Seniors Head 1 in 5 Households

U.S. households headed by people over age 65: 1 in 5.[1]

Number of households headed by older adults: 20 million.[2]

Percentage of senior householders between age 65 and 74: 59.[3]

Percentage 75 and over: 41.[4]

Increase in senior households from 1970 to 1989: 7 million.[5]

Owning vs. Renting

Owning

Households headed by older persons that are owner-occupied: 3 in 4.[6]

Percentage of owner-occupied elderly houses that are owned free and clear: 83.[7]

Percentage of persons age 65 to 74 who have a mortgage on their home: 18.[8]

Percentage of persons 75 and over: 5.[9]

The median value for senior owner-occupied housing in 1985: $52,281.[10]

Percentage of seniors living in housing structures built before 1950: 44.[11]

The median value of senior-occupied houses built between 1940 and 1949: $49,218.[12]

Percentage of senior households with new construction between 1981 and 1985: 3.[13]

The median value of houses with new construction between 1981 and 1985: $73,778.[14]

Renting

Senior households that are rental units: 1 in 4.[15]

Percentage of persons age 65 to 74 who are renters: 22.[16]

Percentage of persons age 75 and over: 30.[17]

Percentage of older renters who live in rent-controlled units: 5.[18]

Percentage of householders over age 70 who can afford some form of rental retirement housing: 46.[19]

Number of householders over age 70 who can afford monthly rental payments of over $1,200 for a one-person household or $1,500 for a two-person household: 2.2 million.[20]

Number of seniors receiving rent reductions by living in public housing developments or in housing covered by some form of federal, state, or local government rent subsidy: 1.5 million.[21]

Estimated shortage of rental housing for seniors per year during the 1990s: 300,000 units.[22]

Housing and Living Arrangements

Most Seniors Live in Single Detached Homes

Percentage of seniors living in single detached homes: 65.[23]

Percentage living in single attached homes: 4.[24]

Percentage living in buildings with two or more units: 26.[25]

Percentage living in a condominium or cooperative: 4.[26]

Percentage living in mobile homes or trailers: 5.[27]

The median number of bedrooms in senior households: 2.6.[28]

The percentage of senior households with no bathrooms: 1.[29]

Number of retirees living in continuing care retirement communities (with an average age of 82): 210,000.[30]

Seniors in Public and Assisted Housing

Percentage of public housing units occupied by seniors in 1988: 44.[31]

Number of public housing units occupied by seniors: roughly 540,000.[32]

Number of seniors living in Section 8 assisted housing units (sponsored by the U.S. Department of Housing and Urban Development) in 1988: 983,000.[33]

Number of seniors living in Section 202 units (sponsored by the U.S. Department of Housing and Urban Development): roughly 188,000.[34]

Single Seniors More Likely To Rent

Percentage of seniors living alone who rent: 40.[35]

Percentage of seniors living with others who rent: 16.[36]

Percentage of senior households owned by older men or women living alone: 37.[37]

Percentage of rented units occupied by seniors living alone: 68.[38]

Housing Problems

High Cost of Housing

Senior households that spend 30 percent or more of their income on housing: 3 in 4 (74 percent).[39]

The percentage spending at least 50 percent of their income on housing: 44.[40]

Senior renters with very low incomes who do not receive public assistance: almost half. (Very low income senior renters have incomes below 50 percent of the median income for their area.)[41]

Housing Flaws

Percentage of senior housing units that have "physical problems": 8. (Physical problems are flaws in one or more of six areas: plumbing, kitchen, maintenance of physical structure, public hall/common area, heating, or electrical system.) [42]

Percentage of older blacks and Hispanics who live in housing with physical problems compared to older whites: 27 percent of older blacks and 19 percent of older Hispanics compared to 6 percent of older whites.[43]

Percentage of older rural householders who live in inadequate housing compared to older urban householders: 13 percent for older rural householders compared to 6 percent of older urban householders.[44]

Percentage of seniors who say they sometimes go without heat in the winter when they need it: 4, representing over 1 million seniors.[45]

Around the House

Housework

Percentage of persons over age 50 who do repair/work around the house: 67.[46]

Percentage who do garden or lawn work: 68.[47]

Percentage who say they give gardening and landscaping a high priority: 42.[48]

Percentage who say they have a strong need to keep up with the latest trends in home decorating: 20.[49]

The number of hours per week that women age 51 to 65 spend cooking and cleaning: 21.5 hours.[50]

Compared to men in the same age group: 13.1 hours.[51]

Home Appliances and Accessories

Percentage of persons over age 50 who own a microwave: 62.[52]

Percentage who own a portable cassette tape player: 40.[53]

Percentage who own a videocassette recorder (VCR): 34.[54]

Percentage who own an answering machine: 11.[55]

Percentage who give a high priority to home furnishings: 42.[56]

Percentage of seniors in 1987 who had recently purchased a food processor: 16.[57]

Percentage who had purchased a coffee grinder: 7.[58]

Percentage who had purchased a dishwasher: 5.[59]

Percentage who had purchased a refrigerator: 8.[60]

Some Seniors Lack Phones

Percentage of older renters who are without telephones: 9.[61]

Percentage of older homeowners: 4.[62]

Choosing Where To Live

Where Seniors Want To Live

Percentage of seniors who say they want to remain in their present homes: 78.[63]

Percentage of seniors who say they plan to move to another home upon retirement: 35.[64]

Percentage of seniors who want to live with their children: 4.[65]

Percentage who want their children to live with them: under 7.[66]

Percentage who find continuing care retirement communities appealing: 45.[67]

Percentage who say they like best the choice of assisted living, such as hiring help for household chores so that they can stay in their own homes: 65.[68]

But, in another survey conducted for the American Association of Retired Persons, the portion of people 55 or older who report that they have given little thought to their future housing needs: more than half.[69]

The percentage who have consulted no one—family, friends or professionals—about where they'll live in retirement: 88.[70]

And the percentage of those over 60 who say they don't ever want to move: 86.[71]

Where Adults in General Say Seniors Should Live

Percentage of adults who think that seniors should live with their children when they cannot take care of themselves: 43.[72]

Percentage who think they should live in senior citizen housing or nursing homes: 24.[73]

Percentage who are not sure: 33.[74]

Most Adult Children Would Have Parents Live with Them

Percentage of children who think their older parents should live with them if they are no longer capable of living alone: 75.[75]

Percentage of children who feel that their older dependent parents should *not* live with them: 14.[76]

Notes

1. U.S. Bureau of the Census, *Households,* 1989: 5.
2. U.S. Bureau of the Census, *Households,* 1989: 5.
3. U.S. Bureau of the Census, *Households,* 1989: 5.
4. U.S. Bureau of the Census, *Households,* 1989: 5.
5. U.S. Bureau of the Census, *Households,* 1989: 5.
6. U.S. Department of Commerce, *American Housing Survey,* 1988: 332.
7. U.S. Department of Commerce, *American Housing Survey,* 1988: 332.
8. U.S. Department of Labor Consumer Expenditure Survey. Reported in *Mature Market Report,* September 1988: 6.
9. U.S. Department of Labor Consumer Expenditure Survey. Reported in *Mature Market Report,* September 1988: 6.
10. U.S. Department of Commerce, *American Housing Survey,* 1988: 342.
11. U.S. Department of Commerce, *American Housing Survey,* 1988: 10.
12. U.S. Department of Commerce, *American Housing Survey,* 1988: 342.
13. U.S. Department of Commerce, *American Housing Survey,* 1988: 288.
14. U.S. Department of Commerce, *American Housing Survey,* 1988: 320.
15. U.S. Department of Commerce, *American Housing Survey,* 1988: 332.
16. U.S. Department of Labor Consumer Expenditure Survey. Reported in *Mature Market Report,* September 1988: 6.
17. U.S. Department of Labor Consumer Expenditure Survey. Reported in *Mature Market Report,* September 1988: 6.
18. U.S. Department of Commerce, *American Housing Survey,* 1988: 314.
19. *Mature Market Report,* November 1987: 7.
20. *Mature Market Report,* November 1987: 7.
21. U.S. Department of Commerce, *American Housing Survey,* 1988: 36.
22. Data are from the University of Michigan National Center on Housing and Living Arrangements for Older Americans. Reported in *Older Americans Reports,* June 24, 1988.
23. U.S. Department of Commerce, *American Housing Survey,* 1988: 10.
24. U.S. Department of Commerce, *American Housing Survey,* 1988: 10.
25. U.S. Department of Commerce, *American Housing Survey,* 1988: 10.
26. U.S. Department of Commerce, *American Housing Survey,* 1988: 10.

27. U.S. Department of Commerce, *American Housing Survey,* 1988: 10.

28. U.S. Department of Commerce, *American Housing Survey,* 1988: 342.

29. U.S. Department of Commerce, *American Housing Survey,* 1988: 342.

30. *Older Americans Reports,* December 22, 1989: 493.

31. U.S. Senate Special Committee on Aging, *Developments in Aging 1988,* 1989: 269.

32. U.S. Senate Special Committee on Aging, *Developments in Aging 1988,* 1989: 269.

33. U.S. Senate Special Committee on Aging, *Developments in Aging 1988,* 1989: 269.

34. U.S. Senate Special Committee on Aging, *Developments in Aging 1988,* 1989: 269.

35. U.S. Department of Commerce, *American Housing Survey,* 1988: 304.

36. U.S. Department of Commerce, *American Housing Survey,* 1988: 304.

37. U.S. Department of Commerce, *American Housing Survey,* 1988: 304.

38. U.S. Department of Commerce, *American Housing Survey,* 1988: 304.

39. Study by the Center on Budget and Policy Priorities and the Low Income Housing Information Service. Reported in *Older Americans Reports,* April 21, 1989: 156.

40. Study by the Center on Budget and Policy Priorities and the Low Income Housing Information Service. Reported in *Older Americans Reports,* April 21, 1989: 156.

41. Study by the Center on Budget and Policy Priorities and the Low Income Housing Information Service. Reported in *Older Americans Reports,* April 21, 1989: 156.

42. U.S. Department of Commerce, *American Housing Survey,* 1988: 300.

43. U.S. Senate Special Committee on Aging, *Aging America,* 1989: 118.

44. U.S. Department of Commerce, *American Housing Survey,* 1988: 288.

45. Harris, 1986: 44.

46. Daniel Yankelovich Group, 1987: 15.

47. Daniel Yankelovich Group, 1987: 15.

48. Daniel Yankelovich Group, 1987: 14.

49. Daniel Yankelovich Group, 1987: 14.

50. *Mature Market Report,* February 1989: 9.

51. *Mature Market Report,* February 1989: 9.

52. Daniel Yankelovich Group, 1987: 20.

53. Daniel Yankelovich Group, 1987: 20.

54. Daniel Yankelovich Group, 1987: 20.

55. Daniel Yankelovich Group, 1987: 20.

56. Daniel Yankelovich Group, 1987: 20.

57. Data are from Mediamark Research Inc. Reported in *Mature Market Report,* December 1987: 5.

58. Data are from Mediamark Research Inc. Reported in *Mature Market Report,* December 1987: 5.

59. Data are from Mediamark Research Inc. Reported in *Mature Market Report,* December 1987: 5.

60. Data are from Mediamark Research Inc. Reported in *Mature Market Report,* December 1987: 5.

61. U.S. Department of Commerce, *American Housing Survey,* 1988: 300.

62. U.S. Department of Commerce, *American Housing Survey,* 1988: 300.
63. Survey conducted for the American Association of Retired Persons (AARP). Reported in *Older Americans Reports,* June 5, 1987: 9.
64. Survey of 1,000 adults conducted by New World Decisions for Transamerica Life Companies. Transamerica Life Companies, 1988: 7.
65. Survey of 1,000 adults conducted by New World Decisions for Transamerica Life Companies. Transamerica Life Companies, 1988: 7.
66. Survey of 1,000 adults conducted by New World Decisions for Transamerica Life Companies. Transamerica Life Companies, 1988: 7.
67. Survey of 1,000 adults conducted by New World Decisions for Transamerica Life Companies. Transamerica Life Companies, 1988: 7.
68. Survey of 1,000 adults conducted by New World Decisions for Transamerica Life Companies. Transamerica Life Companies, 1988: 7.
69. Peterson, 1990: D1.
70. Peterson, 1990: D1.
71. Peterson, 1990: D1.
72. Data are from a national public opinion poll conducted for *Parents* magazine. Reported in Groller, 1989: 31.
73. Data are from a national public opinion poll conducted for *Parents* magazine. Reported in Groller, 1989: 31.
74. Data are from a national public opinion poll conducted for *Parents* magazine. Reported in Groller, 1989: 31.
75. Data are from a national public opinion poll conducted for *Parents* magazine. Reported in Groller, 1989: 31.
76. Data are from a national public opinion poll conducted for *Parents* magazine. Reported in Groller, 1989: 31.

Chapter 9

Transportation

Getting Around

Most Seniors Rely on Cars for Transportation

Percentage of person trips that are by private vehicle for persons age 65 to 74: 86.[1]

Percentage by public transportation: 3.[2]

Percentage by taxi: less than 1.[3]

Percentage by walking: 10.[4]

Percentage of person-trips that are by private vehicle for persons over age 85: 79.[5]

Percentage by public transportation: 4.[6]

Percentage by taxi: 0.[7]

Percentage by walking: 14.[8]

The average length of a walking trip by seniors: less than one-third of a mile.[9]

Most Seniors Own Cars

The percentage of older households with no car, truck, or van: 26.[10]

The percentage with at least one car (with or without a truck or van): 54.[11]

The percentage of persons over 50 who give a high priority to automobiles: 55.[12]

The status car in Sun City, Arizona, where the median age of the population is 69: the Cadillac.[13]

While Most Seniors Rely on Cars, Driving Declines with Age

The percentage of seniors who have a driver's license: 62.[14]

The percentage of persons age 65 to 69 who have a driver's license compared to persons over 85: 75 versus 22.[15]

The increase in licensure for senior women from 1969 to 1983: from 26 to 49 percent.[16]

Age group that logs the fewest miles as drivers and passengers in cars: drivers over 70.[17]

Average miles driven in 1983 by persons age 65 to 69 compared to the oldest-old: 6,804 versus 1,053.[18]

Men and Women behind the Wheel

Across all age groups the segment of the population that drives the most miles per year: men.[19]

Across all age groups the segment that is most likely to be involved in a car crash: male drivers are 3.5 times more likely.[20]

On the basis of miles driven the age after which driver fatalities are the same for men and women: after age 50.[21]

Travel Safety

Traffic Deaths

Every day in the United States: 16 seniors are killed in automobile accidents.[22]

Deaths of seniors as a percentage of all traffic deaths in 1986: 13.[23]

Number of seniors killed in motor vehicle crashes in 1986: 5,900.[24]

The portion of these fatalities that were persons over age 75: half.[25]

Proportion that were pedestrians: one-fourth.[26]

Age group with the highest rate of fatalities from pedestrian accidents: persons over 65.[27]

Comparing Old and Young

Highest rates of senior injuries for drivers: the oldest and youngest drivers have the highest rates.[28]

Probability of dying of an automobile accident for a victim over age 65 versus a 20-year-old if both have serious injuries of equal severity: the senior is three times more likely to die.[29]

The likelihood of a driver over 69 being in a fatal crash compared to middle-aged drivers: twice as likely.[30]

The percentage of all fatalities from traffic deaths in 2020 that are expected to be seniors: 17.[31]

Percentage of automobile trips by seniors that are made at night compared with those made by younger drivers: 13 versus 25.[32]

Failure To Yield and Turns Are Major Accident Causes

The likelihood of a driver over age 65 being in a fatal crash because of failure to yield the right of way compared to a driver under age 65: over three times more likely.[33]

The age group that is overrepresented in crashes that involve turning from either the right- or left-hand lane: older drivers.[34]

The age group that is least likely to be in accidents due to speeding and drinking and driving: older drivers.[35]

The measure that results in fewer accidents and traffic violations for older drivers: completing a driver education course.[36]

Notes

1. Data for 1983. Transportation Research Board, 1988: 29.
2. Data for 1983. Transportation Research Board, 1988: 29.
3. Data for 1983. Transportation Research Board, 1988: 29.
4. Data for 1983. Transportation Research Board, 1988: 29.
5. Data for 1983. Transportation Research Board, 1988: 29.
6. Data for 1983. Transportation Research Board, 1988: 29.
8. Data for 1983. Transportation Research Board, 1988: 29.
8. Data for 1983. Transportation Research Board, 1988: 29.
9. Data for 1983. Transportation Research Board, 1988: 29.
10. U.S. Department of Commerce, *American Housing Survey,* 1988: 22.
11. U.S. Department of Commerce, *American Housing Survey,* 1988: 22.
12. Daniel Yankelovich Group, 1987: 20.
13. Weiss, *Clustering,* 1988: 134.
14. Data are for 1983. Transportation Research Board, 1988: 26.
15. Data are for 1983. Transportation Research Board, 1988: 105.
16. Transportation Research Board, 1988: 26.
17. Transportation Research Board, 1988: 106.

18. Data are for 1983. Transportation Research Board, 1988: 105.
19. Transportation Research Board, 1988: 41.
20. Transportation Research Board, 1988: 41.
21. Transportation Research Board, 1988: 41.
22. Based on Transportation Research Board, 1988: 35.
23. Transportation Research Board, 1988: 35.
24. Transportation Research Board, 1988: 35.
25. Transportation Research Board, 1988: 35.
26. Transportation Research Board, 1988: 35.
27. Transportation Research Board, 1988: 17.
28. Transportation Research Board, 1988: 44.
29. Transportation Research Board, 1988: 3.
30. Transportation Research Board, 1988: 41.
31. Transportation Research Board, 1988: 16.
32. Transportation Research Board, 1988: 30.
33. Transportation Research Board, 1988: 49.
34. Transportation Research Board, 1988: 49.
35. Transportation Research Board, 1988: 49.
36. Research conducted by the California Department of Motor Vehicles. Reported in *Older Americans Reports,* August 25, 1989: 337.

Chapter 10

Seniors in the Community

At the Polls

Seniors Outvote the Young

Proportion of voters who are seniors: 1 in 5.[1]

Number of seniors who voted in 1988: 20 million.[2]

Americans with the highest voting rates in the last five elections: voters age 55 to 74.[3]

The age group twice as likely to vote as those in the 18 to 19 age group: voters age 55 to 74.[4]

The likelihood that a person over 75 will vote compared to an individual under age 35: the 75-plus person is more likely to vote.[5]

The highest voting rates among blacks: those age 65 to 74.[6]

Men and Women Voters

Percentage of men age 65 to 74 voting in the 1988 election compared to women this age: 75 versus 72.[7]

Percentage of men age 75 voting in the 1988 election compared to women this age: 70 versus 58.[8]

The Community Helping Seniors

Who Uses Community Services

Percentage of persons between the ages of 55 and 79 who have little idea of the range of services for seniors available in their community or are not interested in age-segregated activities: 60.[9]

Percentage of seniors who use at least one community service: 11.[10]

Percentage who use three or more community services: 3.[11]

Percentage who visit senior centers.15.[12]

Percentage who take part in senior center meals: 8.[13]

Percentage who ride on special transportation for the elderly: 4.[14]

Percentage of those living alone who use a community service compared to those living with others: 20 versus 12.[15]

Percentage of those living alone who eat meals at senior centers compared to those living with others: 12 versus 6.[16]

Percentage of those living alone who use special transportation for the elderly compared to those living with others: 11 versus 2.[17]

Few Receive Community Services at Home

Percentage who receive home-delivered meals: 2.[18]

Percentage who receive homemaker services: 1.[19]

Percentage who receive services from visiting nurses: 3.[20]

Percentage who receive services from home health aides: 3.[21]

Seniors Helping the Community

Who Volunteers?

Every day in the United States: seniors contribute 163,000 hours of volunteer work.[22]

Percentage of persons age 55 to 64 who volunteer: 47.[23]

Percentage age 65 to 74: 40.[24]

Percentage age 75 and over: 29.[25]

Percentage of seniors who say they were asked to volunteer in the past year and they said no: 23.[26]

Of these the percentage who said no for health reasons: 37.[27]

Percentage who said no because they were too busy: 24.[28]

Average number of hours per week persons age 55 to 64 volunteer: 5.[29]

Average number of hours per week for persons age 65 to 74: 6.[30]

Average number of hours per week for persons age 75 and over: 4.[31]

Proportion of chief executive officers from the country's largest corporations who in 1984 had retired in the last two years and who were volunteers: more than one third.[32]

Where Seniors Volunteer

Where the majority of seniors volunteer: religious groups.[33]

Percentage of seniors who volunteer for religious groups: 66.[34]

Percentage for community service activities: 42.[35]

Percentage for social service agencies: 27.[36]

Percentage for youth agencies: 20.[37]

Percentage for other groups: 35.[38]

In a 1985 survey the number of companies identified that encourage retiree involvement in volunteer activities: 150.[39]

Percentage of Red Cross donors who are older than 50: 62.[40]

Why Seniors Volunteer

Percentage of seniors who say they volunteer because they thought they would enjoy the work: 40.[41]

Percentage who wanted to do something useful: 56.[42]

Percentage who wanted to learn, get experience: 6.[43]

Percentage who thought a family member or friend would benefit: 11.[44]

Percentage who previously benefited from the activity: 5.[45]

Percentage who volunteered because of religious concerns: 27.[46]

Percentage who volunteered because they had a lot of free time: 14.[47]

Percentage who had other reasons or didn't know why they volunteered: 6.[48]

Volunteers in Federal Programs

Number of older volunteers participating in the federal Retired Senior Volunteer Program (RSVP): 402,200 by the end of the 1990 fiscal year.[49]

Number of hours RSVP volunteers contribute per year: 73.3 million hours at an estimated value of $242 million.[50]

Number of seniors participating in the federal Foster Grandparent program: 27,700 low-income seniors.[51]

Number of children helped through the Foster Grandparent program on a given day: 70,000.[52]

Number of volunteer service years in the Senior Companion Program: 7,600.[53]

Helping Friends, Neighbors, and Relatives

Percentage of persons age 65 to 74 living alone who help friends, neighbors, or relatives: 65.[54]

Percentage of couples age 65 to 74 who help: 72.[55]

Percentage of persons 75 and over living alone who help friends, neighbors, or relatives: 40.[56]

Percentage of couples 75 and over: 53.[57]

Helping with Dollars

Age group that contributes the most to charity: retirees.[58]

Percentage of persons age 55 to 64 who contribute money to charity: 79.[59]

Percentage age 65 to 74: 72.[60]

Percentage age 75 and over: 75.[61]

Average contribution for persons age 55 to 64: $959.[62]

For persons age 65 to 74: $737.[63]

For persons over age 75: $219.[64]

Staying Involved

Community Involvement

Percentage of seniors who are very active in their communities: 10.[65]

Percentage who are fairly active: 16.[66]

Percentage who are somewhat active: 23.[67]

Joining Together

Members of the American Association of Retired Persons (AARP): 30 million.[68]

The proportion of Americans who will be eligible for membership in AARP in 2030: 1 in 3.[69]

Members of the Gray Panthers: 70,000-plus.[70]

Members of the National Alliance of Senior Citizens: 2 million-plus.[71]

Members of the National Committee to Preserve Social Security and Medicare: 5.8 million.[72]

Members of the National Council of Senior Citizens: 4.8 million.[73]

Members of the Older Women's League (OWL): 20,000-plus.[74]

Notes

1. Data are from the 1988 election. U.S. Senate Special Committee on Aging, *Aging America*, 1989: 119–121.
2. U.S. Senate Special Committee on Aging, *Aging America*, 1989: 119–121.
3. U.S. Senate Special Committee on Aging, *Aging America*, 1989: 119–121.
4. U.S. Senate Special Committee on Aging, *Aging America*, 1989: 119–121.
5. U.S. Senate Special Committee on Aging, *Aging America*, 1989: 119–121.
6. Gibson, 1986: 3.
7. U.S. Senate Special Committee on Aging, *Aging America*, 1989: 119–121.
8. U.S. Senate Special Committee on Aging, *Aging America*, 1989: 119–121.
9. Survey by AgeAware. Reported in *Mature Market Report*, May 1989: 3.
10. Data based on use of community services during 1983. National Center for Health Statistics, *Aging in the Eighties*, 1986: 2.
11. Data based on use of community services during 1983. National Center for Health Statistics, *Aging in the Eighties*, 1986: 2.
12. Data based on use of community services during 1983. National Center for Health Statistics, *Aging in the Eighties*, 1986: 2.
13. Data based on use of community services during 1983. National Center for Health Statistics, *Aging in the Eighties*, 1986: 2.
14. Data based on use of community services during 1983. National Center for Health Statistics, *Aging in the Eighties*, 1986: 2.
15. Data based on use of community services during 1983. National Center for Health Statistics, *Aging in the Eighties*, 1986: 2.
16. Data based on use of community services during 1983. National Center for Health Statistics, *Aging in the Eighties*, 1986: 2.
17. Data based on use of community services during 1983. National Center for Health Statistics, *Aging in the Eighties*, 1986: 2.

18. Data based on use of community services during 1983. National Center for Health Statistics, *Aging in the Eighties,* 1986: 2.

19. Data based on use of community services during 1983. National Center for Health Statistics, *Aging in the Eighties,* 1986: 2.

20. Data based on use of community services during 1983. National Center for Health Statistics, *Aging in the Eighties,* 1986: 2.

21. Data based on use of community services during 1983. National Center for Health Statistics, *Aging in the Eighties,* 1986: 2.

22. Based on Independent Sector, 1988: 13.

23. Independent Sector, 1988: 13.

24. Independent Sector, 1988: 13.

25. Independent Sector, 1988: 13.

26. Independent Sector, 1988: 34.

27. Independent Sector, 1988: 35.

28. Independent Sector, 1988: 35.

29. Independent Sector, 1988: 13.

30. Independent Sector, 1988: 13.

31. Independent Sector, 1988: 13.

32. Survey conducted by Russell Reynolds Associates. Reported in United Way, 1988: 25.

33. United Way, 1988: 25.

34. United Way, 1988: 25.

35. United Way, 1988: 25.

36. United Way, 1988: 25.

37. United Way, 1988: 25.

38. United Way, 1988: 25.

39. United Way, 1988: 25.

40. *Mature Market Report,* December 1987.

41. Independent Sector, 1988: 29.

42. Independent Sector, 1988: 29.

43. Independent Sector, 1988: 29.

44. Independent Sector, 1988: 29.

45. Independent Sector, 1988: 29.

46. Independent Sector, 1988: 29.

47. Independent Sector, 1988: 29.

48. Independent Sector, 1988: 29.

49. The volunteer programs in this section are run by the federal ACTION Agency. RSVP volunteers work in local communities in a full range of positions from children's daycare centers to hospitals. Foster Grandparents are low-income seniors who assist children who have special needs. The Senior Companion Program is similar to the Foster Grandparent program except that low income seniors assist other seniors in nursing homes, hospitals, or their own homes. *Older Americans Reports,* April 7, 1989: 136.

50. *Older Americans Reports,* April 7, 1989: 136.

51. *Older Americans Reports,* April 7, 1989: 136.

52. *Older Americans Reports,* April 7, 1989: 136.

53. *Older Americans Reports,* April 7, 1989: 136.

54. The Commonwealth Fund Commission on Elderly People Living Alone, 1988: 77.

55. The Commonwealth Fund Commission on Elderly People Living Alone, 1988: 77.
56. The Commonwealth Fund Commission on Elderly People Living Alone, 1988: 77.
57. The Commonwealth Fund Commission on Elderly People Living Alone, 1988: 77.
58. Independent Sector, 1988: 21.
59. Independent Sector, 1988: 13.
60. Independent Sector, 1988: 13.
61. Independent Sector, 1988: 13.
62. Independent Sector, 1988: 13.
63. Independent Sector, 1988: 13.
64. Independent Sector, 1988: 13.
65. Independent Sector, 1988: 53.
66. Independent Sector, 1988: 53.
67. Independent Sector, 1988: 53.
68. Dychtwald, 1989: 55.
69. American Association for International Aging, 1989: 271.
70. American Association for International Aging, 1989: 271.
71. American Association for International Aging, 1989: 297.
72. American Association for International Aging, 1989: 86.
73. American Association for International Aging, 1989: 89.
74. American Association for International Aging, 1989: 95.

Chapter 11

Leisure, Religion, and Travel

Leisure

Seniors Participate Socially

Percentage of seniors who visit friends three or more times a week: 59.[1]

Percentage who regularly attend parties and social gatherings: 57.[2]

Percentage of persons age 65 to 74 who attend at least one classical music performance in a year: 13.[3]

Percentage attending at least one play: 10.[4]

Percentage attending at least one musical play in a year: 13.[5]

Percentage attending at least one jazz performance, one opera performance, or one ballet: 3, 3, and 4, respectively.[6]

Percentage visiting an art museum or gallery at least once a year: 16.[7]

Seniors Stay Informed

Percentage of seniors reading at least one novel, short story, poetry collection, or play in a year: 50.[8]

Percentage who read the newspaper: 82.[9]

Percentage of seniors who are nonreaders: 10.[10]

Percentage who watch television: 95.[11]

Percentage who listen to the radio: 66.[12]

Three magazines that the residents of Sun City, Arizona, read at twice the national average: *Tennis, Boating,* and *Golf Digest.*[13]

Seniors Participate in Sports

Percentage of seniors who fish or hunt: 14.[14]

The percentage of all rounds of golf played by seniors: 32 percent. (They also generate 46 percent of all golf spending.)[15]

The number of rounds of golf played in 1984 by the residents of Sun City, Arizona, where the median age is 69: 1 million.[16]

The number of senior athletes who participated in the local qualifying games for the 1989 Second Biennial National Senior Olympics: 200,000.[17] (In future games the Senior Olympics will be called the National Senior Sports Classic.)

The number of senior athletes registered to participated in the 1989 Second Biennial National Senior Olympics in St. Louis: 3,500.[18]

The number of persons 80 and over who participate in the Second Biennial National Senior Olympics: 162.[19]

The oldest participant in the games: age 91.[20]

The number of seniors participating in track and field events: 1,300.[21]

The number of senior athletes participating in U.S. National Senior Olympics annual member game events: 100,000.[22]

Males as a percentage of Senior Olympics participants: 63.[23]

Females as a percentage of Senior Olympics participants: 37.[24]

Percentage of the 1989 New York City Marathon runners who were age 50 and over: 12.[25]

Number who were 60 and over: 400.[26]

Number who were 90 and over: 3.[27]

Seniors Participate in the Computer Age

Number of seniors using computers at home in 1984: 26,607.[28]

Percentage using computers for video games: 19.[29]

Percentage using them for household records: 50.[30]

Percentage using them for job-related reasons: 18.[31]

Percentage using them for word processing: 21.[32]

Percentage learning to use them: 61.[33]

Median number of days per week seniors with home computers use them: 3.[34]

Religion

Seniors Benefit from Religion

The most frequently mentioned way of coping with stressful life events for older people with high socioeconomic and educational status: religious practices such as praying and obtaining help and strength from God.[35]

Percentage of adults over 50 who devote time to religion: 50.[36]

Going Places

Seniors on the Move

Percentage of all passport holders who are over age 55: 44.[37]

Percentage of adults over age 50 who say that they have a strong need to do things to enrich life such as travel: 44.[38]

Percentage who say they pay more attention to taking trips to interesting places: 34.[39]

Percentage of summer travelers who are seniors: 11.[40]

Percentage of fall travelers: 12.[41]

Most Seniors Travel for Pleasure

Percentage of seniors who say they travel for pleasure: 85.[42]

Percentage traveling for business: 10.[43]

Seniors Bolster Travel Industry

Percentage of all travelers who are seniors: 22.[44]

Percentage of all commercial vacation travel by seniors: almost 80.[45]

Percentage of cruise travelers who are seniors: 60.[46]

Percentage of golfing vacationers: 57.[47]

Percentage of domestic travelers: 30.[48]

Percentage of all package-inclusive tour travelers: 32.[49]

Percentage of people over 50 who take escorted tours: 20.[50]

Where They Go

The top five vacation choices for adults over 50: national parks, historical sites, beaches and other warm weather destinations, fall foliage tours, and special events and festivals.[51]

Percentage who take a vacation in the United States each year: 69.[52]

Percentage who travel abroad: 5.[53]

Percentage who take round trips under 300 miles: 28.[54]

Where They Stay

Percentage of seniors who stay with friends or relatives during travel: 40.[55]

Percentage staying in hotels and motels: 38.[56]

How They Get There

Percentage traveling in groups of four or more: 3.[57]

Percentage of trips by seniors in which an automobile is the mode of transportation: more than 80.[58]

Percentage of all recreational vehicle (RV) trips that are made by seniors: 72.[59]

Percentage of seniors who ride buses: 5.[60]

Millions of nights away from home seniors were predicted to spend in the summer of 1989: 330.[61]

How Much They Spend

Total amount seniors presently spend annually on travel: $51 million.[62]

Total amount seniors are expected to spend by 1995: $56 million.[63]

By 2030: $65 millon.[64]

Notes

1. Harris, 1987: 43.
2. *Mature Market Report,* April, 1988: 10.
3. Data are from the U.S. National Endowment for the Arts, 1985 Survey of Public Participation in the Arts. Reported in U.S. Bureau of the Census, *Statistical Abstract 1989,* 1989: 231.
4. Data are from the U.S. National Endowment for the Arts, 1985 Survey of Public Participation in the Arts. Reported in U.S. Bureau of the Census, *Statistical Abstract 1989,* 1989: 231.
5. Data are from the U.S. National Endowment for the Arts, 1985 Survey of Public Participation in the Arts. Reported in U.S. Bureau of the Census, *Statistical Abstract 1989,* 1989: 231.
6. Data are from the U.S. National Endowment for the Arts, 1985 Survey of Public Participation in the Arts. Reported in U.S. Bureau of the Census, *Statistical Abstract 1989,* 1989: 231.
7. Data are from the U.S. National Endowment for the Arts, 1985 Survey of Public Participation in the Arts. Reported in U.S. Bureau of the Census, *Statistical Abstract 1989,* 1989: 231.
8. Data are from the U.S. National Endowment for the Arts, 1985 Survey of Public Participation in the Arts. Reported in U.S. Bureau of the Census, *Statistical Abstract 1989,* 1989: 231.
9. Data are from Mediamark Research Inc. Reported in U.S. Bureau of the Census, *Statistical Abstract 1989,* 1989: 544.
10. Data are from the 1983 Consumer Research Study on Reading and Book Purchasing. Reported in U.S. Bureau of the Census, *Statistical Abstract 1989,* 1989: 223.
11. Data are from Mediamark Research Inc. Reported in U.S. Bureau of the Census, *Statistical Abstract 1989,* 1989: 544.
12. Data are from Mediamark Research Inc. Reported in U.S. Bureau of the Census, *Statistical Abstract 1989,* 1989: 544.
13. Weiss, *Clustering,* 1988: 56.
14. Data are from the 1985 National Survey of Fishing, Hunting, and Wildlife-Associated Recreation. Reported in U.S. Bureau of the Census, *Statistical Abstract 1989,* 1989: 230.
15. *Golf Shop Operations Magazine.* Reported in *Mature Market Report,* August/September 1989: 7.
16. Weiss, *Clustering,* 1988: 55–56.
17. Data are from the U.S. National Senior Olympics. St. Louis, Misssouri.
18. Data are from the U.S. National Senior Olympics. St. Louis, Missouri.
19. Data are from the U.S. National Senior Olympics. St. Louis, Missouri.
20. Data are from the U.S. National Senior Olympics. St. Louis, Missouri.
21. Data are from the U.S. National Senior Olympics. St. Louis, Missouri.
22. Data are from the U.S. National Senior Olympics. St. Louis, Missouri.
23. Data are from the U.S. National Senior Olympics. St. Louis, Missouri.
24. Data are from the U.S. National Senior Olympics. St. Louis, Missouri.
25. Weinberg, December 1989: 18.
26. Weinberg, December 1989: 18.

27. Weinberg, December 1989: 18.
28. U.S. Bureau of the Census, *Computer Use,* 1988: 16.
29. U.S. Bureau of the Census, *Computer Use,* 1988: 16.
30. U.S. Bureau of the Census, *Computer Use,* 1988: 16.
31. U.S. Bureau of the Census, *Computer Use,* 1988: 16.
32. U.S. Bureau of the Census, *Computer Use,* 1988: 16.
33. U.S. Bureau of the Census, *Computer Use,* 1988: 16.
34. U.S. Bureau of the Census, *Computer Use,* 1988: 16.
35. *Mature Market Report,* July 1988: 7.
36. Daniel Yankelovich Group, 1987: 14.
37. *Mature Market Report,* March 1989: 1.
38. Daniel Yankelovich Group, 1987: 14.
39. Daniel Yankelovich Group, 1987: 14.
40. *Mature Market Report,* August 1988: 7.
41. *Mature Market Report,* August 1988: 7.
42. Data are from the Travel Data Center. Reported in *Mature Market Report,* December 1988: 6.
43. Data are from the Travel Data Center. Reported in *Mature Market Report,* December 1988: 6.
44. *Mature Market Report,* January 1988: 4.
45. *Mature Market Report,* January 1988: 4.
46. *Mature Market Report,* January 1988: 4.
47. *Mature Market Report,* January 1988: 4.
48. *Mature Market Report,* January 1988: 4.
49. *Mature Market Report,* January 1988: 4.
50. Study by Donnelly Marketing and the Mature Market Network. Reported in *Mature Market Report,* June/July 1989: 7.
51. Study by Donnelly Marketing and the Mature Market Network. Reported in *Mature Market Report,* June/July 1989: 7.
52. Based on data from the year prior to the fall of 1987. Daniel Yankelovich Group, 1987: 15.
53. Data are from the Travel Data Center. Reported in *Mature Market Report,* December 1988: 6.
54. Data are from the Travel Data Center. Reported in *Mature Market Report,* December 1988: 6.
55. Data are from the Travel Data Center. Reported in *Mature Market Report,* December 1988: 6.
56. Data are from the Travel Data Center. Reported in *Mature Market Report,* December 1988: 6.
57. Data are from the Travel Data Center. Reported in *Mature Market Report,* December 1988: 6.
58. Transportation Research Board, 1988: 3.
59. *Mature Market Report,* March 1989: 9.
60. Data are from the Travel Data Center and are for the summer of 1987. Reported in *Mature Market Report,* December 1988: 6.
61. *Mature Market Report,* September 1988: 7.
62. *Mature Market Report,* January 1988: 4.
63. *Mature Market Report,* January 1988: 4.
64. *Mature Market Report,* January 1988: 4.

Chapter 12

Seniors and Crime

Senior Crime Victims

Seniors Less Likely To Be Victimized

Percentage of seniors who think crime has gotten worse since they were growing up: 86.[1]

Percentage of seniors who say they worry a lot about being a victim of crime: 15.[2]

The risk that a senior will be a victim of a crime compared to that of younger persons: half.[3]

The one crime that seniors experience as often as other groups: nonforcible purse snatching and pocket picking.[4]

Seniors who experience the highest rates of victimization: males; blacks; divorced and separated persons; and urban residents.[5]

Types of Crimes Committed Against Seniors

Every day in the United States: 432 seniors are victims of violent crimes.[6]

Number of violent crimes per 1,000 seniors: 5.[7]

Number of thefts: 19.[8]

Number of seniors murdered in 1988: 1,123.[9]

Number of senior households per 1,000 with a burglary: 33.[10]

Number with a larceny: 41.[11]

Number with a motor vehicle theft: 4.[12]

Victims of Abuse

Over a Million Seniors May Be Abused

The number of cases of domestic elder abuse in 1988: 2 million.[13]

Perpetrators of abuse who are adult children of the victim: almost 1 in 3 (30 percent).[14]

Percentage of abusers who are spouses: 15 percent.[15]

Percentage who are other relatives such as siblings or grandchildren: 21 percent.[16]

The most common forms of abuse against seniors in order of severity are: neglect, physical abuse, financial/material exploitation, emotional abuse/neglect, and sexual abuse.[17]

Senior Criminals

Seniors in Prison

Prisoners over age 55 who were under a sentence of death in 1987: 39.[18]

Number of 55-plus state prisoners in 1986: 11,000.[19]

Number of 65-plus state prisoners: 3,000.[20]

Number of 55-plus prisoners in all types of prisons: over 20,000.[21]

Number of 85-plus prisoners: more than 400.[22]

Increase in 55-plus prison population: 50 percent every four years.[23]

Percentage of the state prison population who are seniors: less than 1.[24]

Types of Crimes Committed by Seniors

Number of persons over age 65 arrested in 1988: 78,369.[25]

Seniors as a percentage of all arrests: less than 1.[26]

Seniors arrested for violent crimes: 2,941 (compared to a high of 90,964 for persons 25 to 29).[27]

Seniors arrested for murder and nonnegligent manslaughter in 1988: 230.[28]

Seniors arrested for property crimes: 13,179 (compared to a high of 229,819 for persons 25 to 29).[29]

Seniors arrested for forcible rape: 188.[30]

Seniors arrested for robbery and burglary: 455.[31]

Seniors arrested for larceny/theft: 12,595.[32]

Every Day in the United States

Five seniors are arrested for fraud.[33]

Five seniors are arrested for sex offenses.[34]

Eleven seniors are arrested for disorderly conduct.[35]

Thirty-two seniors are arrested for drunkenness.[36]

Notes

1. Weiss, *100%*, 1988 (not paginated).
2. Harris, 1986: 45.
3. Data are from the U.S. Bureau of Justice Statistics, National Crime Survey and are for 1980–1985. Reported in *Older Americans Reports,* December 4, 1987: 10.
4. Data are from the U.S. Bureau of Justice Statistics, National Crime Survey and are for 1980–1985. Reported in *Older Americans Reports,* December 4, 1987: 10.
5. Data are from the U.S. Bureau of Justice Statistics, National Crime Survey and are for 1980–1985. Reported in *Older Americans Reports,* December 4, 1987: 10.
6. Based on data from the U.S. Bureau of Justice Statistics for 1986. Reported in U.S. Bureau of the Census, *Statistical Abstract 1989,* 1989: 170.
7. Data are from the U.S. Bureau of Justice Statistics and are for 1986. Reported in U.S. Bureau of the Census, *Statistical Abstract 1989,* 1989: 170.
8. Data are from the U.S. Bureau of Justice Statistics and are for 1986. Reported in U.S. Bureau of the Census, *Statistical Abstract 1989,* 1989: 170.
9. Federal Bureau of Investigation, 1988: 11.
10. Data are from the U.S. Bureau of Justice Statistics and are for 1986. Reported in U.S. Bureau of the Census, *Statistical Abstract 1989,* 1989: 170.
11. Data are from the U.S. Bureau of Justice Statistics and are for 1986. Reported in U.S. Bureau of the Census, *Statistical Abstract 1989,* 1989: 170.
12. Data are from the U.S. Bureau of Justice Statistics and are for 1986. Reported in U.S. Bureau of the Census, *Statistical Abstract 1989,* 1989: 170.
13. Data are for 1988 and were supplied by the National Aging Resource Center on Elder Abuse.
14. Data are for 1988 and were supplied by the National Aging Resource Center on Elder Abuse.

15. Data are for 1988 and were supplied by the National Aging Resource Center on Elder Abuse.
16. Data are for 1988 and were supplied by the National Aging Resource Center on Elder Abuse.
17. Data are for 1988 and were supplied by the National Aging Resource Center on Elder Abuse.
18. Data are from the U.S. Bureau of Justice Statistics. Reported in U.S. Bureau of the Census, *Statistical Abstract 1989,* 1989: 186.
19. U.S. Bureau of the Census, *Statistical Abstract 1989,* 1989: 183.
20. U.S. Bureau of the Census, *Statistical Abstract 1989,* 1989: 183.
21. Carroll, 1989: 70.
22. Carroll, 1989: 70.
23. American Correctional Association. Reported in *Senior Edition USA,* December 1989: 19.
24. Data are from the U.S. Bureau of Justice Statistics and are for 1986. Reported in U.S. Bureau of the Census, *Statistical Abstract 1989,* 1989: 183.
25. Federal Bureau of Investigation, 1988: 179.
26. Federal Bureau of Investigation, 1988: 179.
27. Federal Bureau of Investigation, 1988: 179.
28. Federal Bureau of Investigation, 1988: 179.
29. Federal Bureau of Investigation, 1988: 179.
30. Federal Bureau of Investigation, 1988: 179.
31. Federal Bureau of Investigation, 1988: 179.
32. Federal Bureau of Investigation, 1988: 179.
33. Based on Federal Bureau of Investigation, 1988: 179.
34. Based on Federal Bureau of Investigation, 1988: 179.
35. Based on Federal Bureau of Investigation, 1988: 179.
36. Based on Federal Bureau of Investigation, 1988: 179.

Chapter 13

Health and Aging

Feeling Good

Majority Feel Healthy

Seniors who view their health as excellent, very good, or good: 7 in 10.[1]

Seniors reporting that their health is fair or poor: 3 in 10.[2]

Seniors with incomes over $35,000 who describe their health as excellent: 1 in 4.[3]

Seniors with incomes below $10,000: slightly more than 1 in 10.[4]

Persons over 80 who say they have no difficulty with walking one-quarter mile, stooping, crouching and kneeling, lifting 10 pounds, or walking ten steps: one-fourth.[5]

Health Habits

Smokers Are a Minority

Portion of persons age 65 to 74 who smoke: 1 in 5 (19 percent).[6]

Portion of those over age 75: 1 in 11 (9 percent).[7]

Percentage age 65 to 74 who are former smokers: 37.[8]

Percentage of those over age 75: 30.[9]

Of smokers age 65 to 74 the portion who smoke more than 35 cigarettes a day: 1 in 10.[10]

Of those over age 75: 1 in 17.[11]

The percentage of seniors who chew tobacco: 3.[12]

The percentage who use snuff: 2.[13]

The percentage who smoke a pipe: 2.[14]

The percentage who smoke cigars: 2.[15]

Most Seniors Moderate Drinkers

Percentage of seniors who never have more than 12 drinks in a year: 22.[16]

Percentage who formerly drank alcohol: 20.[17]

Percentage who currently drink alcohol: 58.[18]

Of current drinkers the portion who are considered heavy drinkers (one or more ounces a day): 1 in 6.[19]

The percentage who say that they have driven when they "perhaps have had too much to drink": 3.[20]

Portion of seniors reporting families with drinking problems: 1 in 5 (21 percent).[21]

Watching the Scale

Percentage of seniors who report that they are very or somewhat overweight: 21.[22]

Portion of seniors who are trying to lose weight by consuming fewer calories: nearly three-fourths.[23]

Portion who exercise to lose weight: slightly over half.[24]

Daily per capita intake of calories by women age 65 to 74: 1,221.[25]

Daily calorie intake for men this age: 1,723.[26]

Sleep and Exercise

Percentage of seniors who sleep less than 6 hours per night: 20.[27]

Portion of 65-plus men who say they exercise or play sports regularly: almost one-third.[28]

Portion of 65-plus women who say they exercise or play sports regularly: over one-fourth.[29]

Percentage of seniors who walk for exercise: 40.[30]

Eating Right

Percentage of seniors who eat breakfast every day: 87.[31]

Percentage of seniors who eat between meals: 55.[32]

Percentage of persons over 50 who say they are now paying attention to eating a more balanced diet: 51.[33]

To eating more fish and poultry: 64.[34]

To watching sugar intake: 51.[35]

To eating more salads: 65.[36]

To using decaffeinated beverages: 37.[37]

To eating less red meat: 33.[38]

To eating more low salt products: 51.[39]

Percentage of seniors who avoid fat: 74.[40]

Percentage who consume fiber: 69.[41]

Percentage who avoid cholesterol: 58.[42]

Percentage who consume vitamins and minerals: 68.[43]

Percentage who consume calcium: 58.[44]

Seniors Not Stressed Out

Portion of seniors who report that stress has little or no effect on their health: nearly two-thirds.[45]

Compared to the portion of younger people: half.[46]

Percentage of seniors who say they take steps to reduce stress: 72.[47]

Preventive Health Practices

Taking Preventive Steps

Age group that is most likely to take steps to prevent or treat a serious illness: seniors.[48]

Percentage of seniors at high risk for pneumococcal infection (the most common form of bacterial pneumonia) who have taken the vaccine that protects against it: 9.[49]

Percentage of high risk seniors who are *not* immunized annually for flu: as many as 80.[50]

Percentage of residents in a retirement community who used regular fecal occult blood tests (recommended yearly after age 50 by the National Cancer Institute): 10.[51]

Keeping Tabs on Blood Pressure

Portion of 65-plus men who have had a blood pressure test in the last year: 8 in 10.[52]

Portion of 65-plus women who have had a blood pressure test in the last year: 9 in 10.[53]

Women and Cancer Detection

Percentage of women in their sixties who had a mammogram in the last year: 14.[54]

Percentage of women in their nineties: 9.[55]

Percentage of women in their sixties who practice breast self-examination: 43.[56]

Percentage of women in their nineties: 25.[57]

Percentage of 65-plus women who had a PAP test in the previous year: 38.[58]

Portion of 65-plus women who have had a breast examination in the last year: 2 in 5.[59]

Car and Home Safety

Portion of seniors who say they usually wear a seat belt: about a third.[60]

Portion of seniors who own one or more smoke detectors: about two-thirds.[61]

Percentage of seniors who avoid smoking in bed: 95.[62]

Percentage who say they take measures to avoid home accidents: 80.[63]

Using Home Medical Tests

Seniors who report using any type of home medical test: 1 in 5.[64]

Percentage who have used blood pressure monitors at home: 14.[65]

Compared to those who say they are interested in using them: 43.[66]

Percentage who express interest in using blood sugar level tests: 35.[67]

In using detection tests: 25.[68]

In using colon cancer tests: 36.[69]

Seniors at Risk

Health Risks High for Seniors

Percentage of persons age 65 to 74 with high-risk serum cholesterol levels: 27.[70]

Percentage with definite or borderline elevated blood pressure: 63.[71]

Percentage with definite elevated blood pressure: 35.[72]

Portion of seniors with clinically identifiable nutrition problems requiring professional intervention: up to half.[73]

Number of years that male life expectancy at age 30 could be increased if major known risk factors such as smoking, cholesterol, high blood pressure, and obesity were eliminated: more than 15 years.[74]

Leading Causes of Death

Heart Disease, Cancer, Strokes Biggest Killers

The chance that an individual over 65 will die from heart disease rather than another condition: twice as high.[75]

The portion of all deaths among the elderly that are from heart disease, cancer, and stroke: three-fourths.[76]

The gain in life expectancy at age 65 if major heart and renal diseases were eliminated: 11 years.[77]

If just heart disease were eliminated: 5 years.[78]

If strokes were eliminated: 1 year.[79]

If cancer were eliminated: 1 year.[80]

Although it is not listed as a cause of death in vital statistics, Alzheimer's disease has been identified by the Alzheimer's Association as: the fourth or fifth leading cause of death.[81]

The leading type of fatal injury for seniors: falls.[82]

Heart Disease Declines, but Is Still Largest Cause of Death

The leading cause of death for seniors: heart disease.[83]

Every day in the United States: 1,729 seniors die from heart disease.[84]

Heart disease as a percentage of all deaths of seniors: 43.[85]

Death rate per 100,000 persons age 65 to 74 for diseases of the heart: 1,020.[86]

The rate per 100,000 persons age 75 to 84: 2,556.[87]

The rate per 100,000 persons over age 85: 7,122.[88]

Decrease in deaths from heart disease over the last 20 years: almost 30 percent.[89]

Women and Heart Disease

The advantage that women have over men in development of heart disease: women develop cardiovascular disease 10 to 20 years later than men.[90]

The percentage of women who have pathological evidence of coronary heart disease by the time they reach their eighties: almost 60.[91]

The likelihood that a woman will suffer a second heart attack within five years of the first compared to the likelihood for a man: two to three times higher.[92]

Men and Heart Disease

The heart of a *healthy* 80-year-old man compared to that of a man in his twenties: it performs about as well.[93]

Percentage of men in their seventies who have pathological evidence of coronary heart disease: between 60 and 75.[94]

Cancer Is Second Largest Killer

The second leading cause of death among seniors: cancer.[95]

Every day in the United States: 915 seniors die of cancer.[96]

Cancer as a percentage of all deaths of seniors: 21.[97]

According to the American Cancer Society the portion of cancers that are preventable: one-half.[98]

Death rate per 100,000 persons age 65 to 74 for malignant neoplasms: 846.[99]

The rate per 100,000 persons age 75 to 84: 1,283.[100]

The rate per 100,000 persons over age 85: 1,632.[101]

The leading cancers: lung, colon, and rectal.[102]

Women and Cancer

Percentage of cancer deaths among senior women that are due to smoking-related cancers: 15.[103]

The leading type of fatal cancer for senior women: breast cancer.[104]

The chance of a woman developing breast cancer after age 65: 1 in 10.[105]

Men and Cancer

Percentage of cancer deaths among senior males that are due to smoking-related cancers: 41.[106]

The likelihood that a man will die of cancer compared to the likelihood for a woman: four times as high.[107]

Strokes Are Third Leading Cause of Death

The third leading cause of death among the elderly: cerebrovascular disease (stroke).[108]

Every day in the United State: 374 seniors die of strokes.[109]

Strokes as a percentage of all deaths of seniors: 9.[110]

Death rate per 100,000 persons age 65 to 74 for cerebrovascular disease: 153.[111]

The rate per 100,000 persons age 75 to 84: 563.[112]

The rate per 100,000 persons over age 85: 1,734.[113]

When Death Comes

A study by the National Institute on Aging found that 53 percent of seniors die in their sleep.[114]

Percentage who are not in pain when they die: 61.[115]

Percentage who die in a hospital: 45.[116]

Percentage who die in a long-term care facility: 25.[117]

Percentage who die at home: 30.[118]

Percentage who are with family members when they die: 89.[119]

Percentage who were thought to be in excellent health a year before they died: 53.[120]

Percentage who had no physical limitations when they died: 59.[121]

Dying of Grief

During the first three months after the death of a spouse, the likelihood that a husband will die as compared to a wife is: 46 percent higher.[122]

Suicide

Suicide Rates High for Seniors

The percentage of all suicides that are by seniors: 17.[123]

Every day in the United States: 19 seniors commit suicide.[124]

The suicide rate per 100,000 persons for the general population: 12.[125]

For persons age 65 to 74: 20.[126]

For persons age 75 to 84: 25.[127]

For persons over 85: 21.[128]

The state with the highest rate of geriatric suicide: Nevada.[129]

Older White Men at Highest Risk for Suicide

The segment of the population that has the highest risk for suicide: older Americans, particularly older white men.[130]

The suicide rate for white men age 65 to 74 is: five times the national rate, four times the rate for older black men, seven times the rate for older white women, and 23 times the rate for older black women.[131]

The suicide rate per 100,000 white males age 65 to 74: 38.[132]

For white males age 75 to 84: 59.[133]

For white males over 85: 66.[134]

Compared to the rate for white women: 8 per 100,00 for those age 65 to 74 and 75 to 84 and 5 for those age 85 and over.[135]

When Illness Strikes

Seniors Are Prone to Acute Illness

Number of acute conditions per 100 seniors per year: 100.[136]

Percentage of seniors' acute conditions that do *not* receive medical attention: 29.[137]

Segment of the population that is most likely to experience acute illnesses that are life threatening: older men.[138]

Average number of annual restricted activity days due to acute conditions for seniors: 8.[139]

Average number of bed disability days: 3.[140]

Most Seniors Suffer from Chronic Conditions

Proportion of seniors with at least one chronic condition: more than four out of five.[141]

The leading chronic conditions for the elderly in rank order: arthritis, hypertensive disease, heart disease, and hearing impairments.[142]

Percentage of persons with chronic disabilities who improved over a two-year period: 22 percent of persons with severe disability and 24 percent of persons with moderate disability.[143]

Older Women Are More Likely To Have Chronic Conditions

Segment of the population that is most likely to experience chronic conditions: older women.[144]

For example, rates for arthritis for senior men and women are 376 per 1,000 versus 564 per 1,000.[145]

And the rates for hypertension for senior men and women are: 305 per 1,000 versus 421 per 1,000.[146]

Arthritis Is the Most Common Chronic Illness

The leading chronic condition for seniors: arthritis.[147]

The rate for arthritis for seniors: 486 per 1,000.[148]

The rate for arthritis for persons age 65 to 74: 445 per 1,000.[149]

The rate for persons 75 and over: 550 per 1,000.[150]

Hypertension Affects More Than One-Third of Seniors

Number of persons over age 55 who have hypertension: over 30 million.[151]

Percentage of senior women with hypertension compared to senior men: 66 versus 59 percent.[152]

The rate for hypertension among seniors: 373 per 1,000.[153]

Osteoporosis Strikes One in Four Senior Women

Proportion of white women over the age of 65 who develop osteoporosis: 1 in 4.[154]

Number of fractures that are estimated to occur each year as a result of the condition: 1.5 million.[155]

Ratio of bone fractures in women compared to men: 4 to 1.[156]

The chance that a 65-plus woman will have a vertebrate fracture: 1 in 3.[157]

Chance of dying within one year after a hip fracture: 1 in 5.[158]

Proportion of those who survive fractures who will require long-term care: half.[159]

The annual cost of fractures resulting from osteoporosis: $7 to $10 billion.[160]

Stage in the life cycle when bone loss accelerates in women: 8 to 10 years after menopause.[161]

Age at which bones are the strongest: the twenties.[162]

The risk for developing osteoporosis for people who smoke: twice the normal rate.[163]

The risk for people who drink alcohol: also twice the normal rate.[164]

Accidents

Accidents Injure One in Five

Every day in the United States: 8,646 seniors are injured at home.[165]

Rate of accidental injuries per 100 seniors per year: 20.[166]

Per 100 65-plus women: 23.[167]

Per 100 65-plus men: 11.[168]

Number of seniors injured in 1988: 5.7 million.[169]

Rate of accidents at home per 100 seniors: 10.[170]

Number of seniors injured at home in 1988: 2.8 million.[171]

Death rate due to motor vehicle accidents per 100,000 persons age 65 to 74: 18.[172]

Per 1,000 persons age 75 to 84: 29.[173]

Per 1,000 persons over 85: 25.[174]

The likelihood of a senior being the victim of a home fire compared to the likelihood for younger persons: two to three times greater.[175]

Falls Are Potential Killers

Proportion of injury-related deaths of persons over age 85 caused by falls: two-thirds.[176]

Of the 8,200 fatal falls for seniors in 1985, the percentage that occurred in the home: 59.[177]

The number of hip fractures per year resulting from falls among persons age 45 and over: 250,000.[178]

Proportion of fatal falls that involve persons over age 75: over one-half.[179]

Percentage of women 55 to 69 who suffer falls: 19 percent.[180]

Among women 70 to 79: 23 percent.[181]

Among women over 80: 34 percent.[182]

Frequency of falls among men age 55 to 69: 15 percent.[183]

Among men 70 to 79: 17 percent.[184]

Among men over 80: 28 percent.[185]

Of seniors reporting a fall, the number who said that they fell more than once: half.[186]

Other Common Health Problems

Dental Problems

The rate at which people over 55 develop cavities compared to the rate for children: twice as high.[187]

Percentage of seniors who have all their teeth: 2.[188]

Percentage of persons age 65 to 74 who are without teeth: 34.[189]

Percentage of persons over age 75: 45.[190]

Percentage of seniors who need full dentures: 9.[191]

Percentage who need partial dentures: 19.[192]

Percentage of seniors who have seen a dentist in the last year: 42.[193]

Percentage who have *not* seen a dentist in two years or more: 51.[194]

Average number of visits to the dentist per senior per year: 2.1.[195]

Vision Problems

Percentage of seniors who wear eyeglasses: 95.[196]

Number of seniors with visual impairment: more than 4 million.[197]

Percentage of seniors with visual impairment: 13.[198]

Percentage with cataracts: 18.[199]

Percentage of persons over age 85: 35.[200]

Percentage of seniors who have had an operation for cataracts: 10.[201]

Percentage over age 85: 21.[202]

Percentage of seniors with blindness in one eye: 3.[203]

Percentage with blindness in both eyes: 1.[204]

Percentage of cataract surgeries that result in the restoration of useful vision: 90 to 95.[205]

Portion of seniors who have glaucoma: 3 in 100.[206]

Visits by seniors as a portion of all visits to physicians for medical eye care: nearly one-third.[207]

Hearing Impairments

Percentage of seniors with a hearing impairment: 29.[208]

Percentage of persons over age 85: 51.[209]

Percentage of seniors with deafness in at least one ear: 7.[210]

Percentage of persons over age 85: 11.[211]

Percentage of seniors using a hearing aid: 8.[212]

Percentage of persons over age 85: 19.[213]

Other Sensory Problems

Number of Americans who are affected by taste and smell disorders: 10 million.[214]

Age after which most of these problems occur: 60: [215]

Percentage of seniors who have major impairments in the ability to smell: 60 percent.[216]

Portion of the taste buds that atrophy by older age: two-thirds.[217]

Women and Menopause

The average age of menopause in 1900: 46 years.[218]

The average age of menopause today: 50 years.[219]

The average portion of the lifespan left for women after menopause: more than one-third.[220]

The portion of senior women who have hot flashes: three-quarters.[221]

Prostate Problems Affect Most Men

Percentage of men over the age of 50 who experience enlargement of the prostate: 80.[222]

Other Health Problems

Number of Americans with Parkinson's disease, many of whom are over age 65: half a million.[223]

Number of diabetics per 1,000 seniors: 92.[224]

Number of persons over age 60 with urinary incontinence: 10 million.[225]

Percentage of seniors with deformity or orthopedic impairment: 16.[226]

Percentage of seniors with chronic sinusitis: 17.[227]

Mental Health

Most Seniors Are Mentally Healthy

Percentage of seniors with serious symptoms of mental disorders: between 15 and 25.[228]

Percentage of state mental hospital patients who are seniors: 27.[229]

Alzheimer's Is the Leading Cause of Cognitive Impairment

The leading cause of cognitive impairment in old age: Alzheimer's disease.[230]

The percentage of seniors who have "probable" Alzheimer's disease: 10.[231] (These and the following estimates of seniors with Alzheimer's disease are controversial. Many analysts think they are inflated. Check with the Alzheimer's Association in Chicago, Illinois, for verification.)

Percentage of persons age 65 to 74 with Alzheimer's disease: 3.[232]

Percentage of persons age 75 to 84: 19.[233]

Percentage of persons over age 85: 47.[234]

Estimated number of cases of Alzheimer's disease in the United States: 4 million.[235]

Projected number of cases of Alzheimer's disease by the middle of the 21st century: 14 million.[236]

Amount of money lost in 1985 due to Alzheimer's disease: $88 billion.[237]

Dementia and Other Cognitive Impairments

Percentage of residents in nursing homes with disorientation or memory impairment: 63.[238]

Percentage with senile dementia or chronic organic brain syndrome: 47.[239]

Percentage of seniors with primary or secondary dementias who reside in the community: 5.[240]

The lifetime risk of dementia for males who survive to 85 years: 1 in 3.[241]

Percentage of seniors who say that the fear of becoming senile and losing their minds is a major worry for them: 12.[242]

Developmentally Disabled Seniors

Portion of developmentally disabled persons who are over age 65 and receiving services: 12 percent.[243]

The number of people over 60 with severe chronic disabilities, many of whom depend for care on parents who themselves need assistance: between 200,000 and 500,000.[244]

Depression, Loneliness, and Anxiety Disorders

Estimated portion of seniors living in the community who suffer from depression of all types: 13 percent.[245]

Estimates of those who suffer from major depression: 1 to 2 percent.[246]

The likelihood that a senior will become depressed compared to the likelihood for a younger person: the likelihood for a senior is twice as high.[247]

The percentage of seniors who reported in a Louis Harris and Associates survey that they feel depressed at least occasionally: 48.[248]

The percentage who said that loneliness is a serious problem for them: 7.[249]

Estimated portion of senior women who suffer from anxiety disorders: 10 percent, with the most common disorders being phobias.[250]

Estimated portion of senior men who suffer from anxiety disorders: about 5 percent.[251]

Portion of seniors who have depression in addition to medical illness: 1 in 7.[252]

In a study of 150 older patients, 15 percent of whom were depressed, the number of physicians who correctly diagnosed depression: none.[253]

Seniors, Drugs, and Alcohol

Alcohol Abuse

Estimated percentage of older Americans who abuse alcohol: 10 to 20.[254]

Of all chronic liver disease and cirrhosis deaths, the percentage that occurs among seniors: 36.[255]

Estimated proportions of life-long alcoholics as opposed to those who become alcoholic after age 60: two-thirds versus one-third.[256]

Drug Use and Abuse

Percentage of all drug use in the United States that is attributed to seniors: 30.[257]

The number of prescriptions that seniors average annually: 15.[258]

The number of prescriptions that persons age 65 to 74 average annually: 14.[259]

The average number for persons over age 75: 17.[260]

Based on a study of 740 participants, the percentage of seniors who are taking at least one prescription drug: over half.[261]

Average number of drugs that people over the age of 60 take simultaneously: 6.[262]

Of these, the ratio of prescription drugs to nonprescription drugs: 5 to 1.[263]

The cost of prescription medicines for noninstitutionalized Medicare beneficiaries: $8.3 billion in 1987.[264]

Percentage of drug takers over age 60 who report at least one side effect: 25.[265]

The most common side effects: urinary frequency and dry mouth.[266]

Percentage of all reported adverse side effects from drugs that are reported by seniors: 26.[267]

The types of drugs most commonly used by seniors: cardiovascular agents and diuretics (36 percent), antiarthritics and analgesics (11 percent), anti-infectives (9 percent), antidiabetics (5 percent), and psychotherapeutics (5 percent).[268]

Of the top 25 drugs prescribed for seniors, the number that are either heart or blood pressure medications: 16.[269]

Of all deaths due to adverse drug reactions, the percentage that are to persons over age 60: 39.[270]

Patients and Doctors Have Drug Communication Gap

Percentage of persons over 60 who say that their physicians told them of possible side effects from a prescribed drug: 8.[271]

Percentage of doctors who say that they told their 60-plus patients about side effects from a prescribed drug: 42.[272]

Notes

1. Does not include persons living in institutions. National Center for Health Statistics, *Current Estimates 1988,* 1989: 114.

2. Does not include persons living in institutions. National Center for Health Statistics, *Current Estimates 1988,* 1989: 114.

3. Does not include persons living in institutions. National Center for Health Statistics, *Current Estimates 1988,* 1989: 114–115.

4. Does not include persons living in institutions. National Center for Health Statistics, *Current Estimates 1988,* 1989: 114–115.

5. *Older Americans Reports,* November 27, 1987: 2.

6. Data are for 1987. National Center for Health Statistics, *Smoking and Tobacco Use,* 1989: 17.

7. Data are for 1987. National Center for Health Statistics, *Smoking and Tobacco Use,* 1989: 17.

8. Data are for 1987. National Center for Health Statistics, *Smoking and Tobacco Use,* 1989: 17.

9. Data are for 1987. National Center for Health Statistics, *Smoking and Tobacco Use,* 1989: 17.

10. Data are for 1987. National Center for Health Statistics, *Smoking and Tobacco Use,* 1989: 17.

11. Data are for 1987. National Center for Health Statistics, *Smoking and Tobacco Use,* 1989: 17.

12. Data are for 1987. National Center for Health Statistics, *Smoking and Tobacco Use,* 1989: 24.

13. Data are for 1987. National Center for Health Statistics, *Smoking and Tobacco Use,* 1989: 26.

14. Data are for 1987. National Center for Health Statistics, *Smoking and Tobacco Use,* 1989: 28.

15. Data are for 1987. National Center for Health Statistics, *Smoking and Tobacco Use,* 1989: 30.

16. Data are for 1985. National Center for Health Statistics, *Adult Health Practices,* 1988: 29.

17. Data are for 1985. National Center for Health Statistics, *Adult Health Practices,* 1988: 29.

18. Data are for 1985. National Center for Health Statistics, *Adult Health Practices,* 1988: 29.

19. Data are for 1985. National Center for Health Statistics, *Adult Health Practices,* 1988: 30.

20. Data are for 1985. National Center for Health Statistics, *Adult Health Practices,* 1988: 30.

21. Harris, 1987: 61.

22. U.S. Department of Health and Human Services, *Databook on the Elderly,* 1987: 60.

23. U.S. Department of Health and Human Services, *Databook on the Elderly,* 1987: 60.

24. U.S. Department of Health and Human Services, *Databook on the Elderly,* 1987: 60.

25. U.S. Bureau of the Census, *Statistical Abstracts 1989,* 1989: 122.

26. U.S. Bureau of the Census, *Statistical Abstracts 1989,* 1989: 122.

27. Data are for 1985. U.S. Bureau of the Census, *Statistical Abstract 1988,* 1987: 111.

28. Data are for 1985. National Center for Health Statistics, *Adult Health Practices,* 1988: 31.

29. Data are for 1985. National Center for Health Statistics, *Adult Health Practices,* 1988: 31.

30. U.S. Department of Health and Human Services, *Databook on the Elderly,* 1987: 60.

31. U.S. Department of Health and Human Services, *Databook on the Elderly,* 1987: 60.

32. U.S. Department of Health and Human Services, *Databook on the Elderly,* 1987: 60.

33. Daniel Yankelovich Group, 1987: 11.

34. Daniel Yankelovich Group, 1987: 11.

35. Daniel Yankelovich Group, 1987: 11.

36. Daniel Yankelovich Group, 1987: 12.

37. Daniel Yankelovich Group, 1987: 12.

38. Daniel Yankelovich Group, 1987: 12.

39. Daniel Yankelovich Group, 1987: 12.

40. Based on a study of 177 persons 65 years of age or older. Bausell, 1986: 557.

41. Based on a study of 177 persons 65 years of age or older. Bausell, 1986: 557.

42. Based on a study of 177 persons 65 years of age or older. Bausell, 1986: 557.

43. Based on a study of 177 persons 65 years of age or older. Bausell, 1986: 557.

44. Based on a study of 177 persons 65 years of age or older. Bausell, 1986: 557.

45. U.S. Department of Health and Human Services, *Databook on the Elderly,* 1987: 60.

46. U.S. Department of Health and Human Services, *Databook on the Elderly,* 1987: 60.

47. Bausell, 1986: 557.

48. Study by Howard Leventhal at Rutgers University. Reported in National Institute on Aging, *Special Report,* 1988: 18.

49. Study by Michael Polis and Richard Kaslow at the National Institute of Neurological and Communicative Disorders. Reported in National Institute on Aging, *Special Report,* 1988: 20.

50. *Mature Market Report,* January 1989: 7.

51. Study by Ronald Ross, Annilia Paganini-Hill, and colleagues at the University of Southern California. Reported in National Institute on Aging, *Special Report,* 1988: 18.

52. Data are for 1985. National Center for Health Statistics, *Adult Health Practices,* 1988: 33.

53. Data are for 1985. National Center for Health Statistics, *Adult Health Practices,* 1988: 33.

54. Study by Ronald Ross, Annilia Paganini-Hill, and colleagues at the University of Southern California. Reported in National Institute on Aging, *Special Report,* 1988: 18.

55. Study by Ronald Ross, Annilia Paganini-Hill, and colleagues at the University of Southern California. Reported in National Institute on Aging, *Special Report,* 1988: 18.

56. Study by Ronald Ross, Annilia Paganini-Hill, and colleagues at the University of Southern California. Reported in National Institute on Aging, *Special Report,* 1988: 18.

57. Study by Ronald Ross, Annilia Paganini-Hill, and colleagues at the University of Southern California. Reported in National Institute on Aging, *Special Report,* 1988: 18.

58. Data are for 1985. National Center for Health Statistics, *Adult Health Practices,* 1988: 34.

59. Data are for 1985. National Center for Health Statistics, *Adult Health Practices,* 1988: 33.

60. Data are for 1985. National Center for Health Statistics, *Adult Health Practices,* 1988: 32.

61. Data are for 1985. National Center for Health Statistics, *Adult Health Practices,* 1988: 32.

62. Bausell, 1986: 557.

63. Bausell, 1986: 557.

64. *Mature Market Report,* July 1988: 3.

65. *Mature Market Report,* July 1988: 3.
66. *Mature Market Report,* July 1988: 3.
67. *Mature Market Report,* July 1988: 3.
68. *Mature Market Report,* July 1988: 3.
69. *Mature Market Report,* July 1988: 3.
70. National Center for Health Statistics, *Health: United States 1988,* 1989: 101.
71. National Center for Health Statistics, *Health: United States 1988,* 1989: 99.
72. National Center for Health Statistics, *Health: United States 1988,* 1989: 100.
73. U.S. Department of Health and Human Services, *Surgeon General's Workshop,* 1988: G-11.
74. Study by Kenneth Manton at Duke University. National Institute on Aging, *Special Report,* 1988: 37.
75. National Institute on Aging, *Answers about Aging,* Fleg, 1988: 1.
76. U.S. Senate Special Committee on Aging, *Aging America,* 1987: 99.
77. Brock, 1984.
78. Brock, 1984.
79. Brock, 1984.
80. Brock, 1984.
81. National Institute on Aging, *Answers about Aging,* Butler, 1988: 4.
82. U.S. Department of Health and Human Services, *Surgeon General's Workshop,* 1988: D-1.
83. U.S. Senate Special Committee on Aging, *Aging America,* 1988: 109.
84. Based on data from the National Center for Health Statistics, reported in U.S. Senate Special Committee on Aging, *Aging America,* 1989: 90.
85. National Center for Health Statistics, *Health Statistics on Older Persons,* 1986: 7, 9.
86. Data are for 1987. National Center for Health Statistics, *Health: United States 1988,* 1989: 78.
87. Data are for 1987. National Center for Health Statistics, *Health: United States 1988,* 1989: 78.
88. Data are for 1987. National Center for Health Statistics, *Health: United States 1988,* 1989: 78.
89. National Institute on Aging, *Answers about Aging,* Fleg, 1988: 1.
90. National Institute on Aging, *The Aging Woman,* undated: 18.
91. National Institute on Aging, *Answers about Aging,* Fleg, 1988: 2.
92. National Institute on Aging, *The Aging Woman,* undated: 19.
93. National Institute on Aging, *The Aging Man,* undated: 5.
94. National Institute on Aging, *Answers about Aging,* Fleg, 1988: 2.
95. U.S. Senate Special Committee on Aging, *Aging America,* 1987: 109.
96. Based on data from the National Center for Health Statistics, reported in U.S. Senate Special Committee on Aging, *Aging America,* 1989: 90.
97. National Center for Health Statistics, Health Statistics on Older Persons, 1986: 7, 12.
98. National Institute on Aging, *The Aging Woman,* undated: 21.
99. Data are for 1987. National Center for Health Statistics, *Health: United States 1988,* 1989: 78.
100. Data are for 1987. National Center for Health Statistics, *Health: United States 1988,* 1989: 78.
101. Data are for 1987. National Center for Health Statistics, *Health: United States 1988,* 1989: 78.

102. National Institute on Aging, *The Aging Man,* undated: 8.

103. U.S. Department of Health and Human Services, *Surgeon General's Workshop,* 1988: I-2.

104. National Institute on Aging, *The Aging Woman,* undated: 21.

105. National Institute on Aging, *The Aging Woman,* undated: 21.

106. U.S. Department of Health and Human Services, *Surgeon General's Workshop,* 1988: I-2.

107. National Institute on Aging, *The Aging Man,* undated: 7.

108. U.S. Senate Special Committee on Aging, *Aging America,* 1987: 110.

109. Based on data from the National Center for Health Statistics, reported in U.S. Senate Special Committee on Aging, *Aging America,* 1989: 90.

110. National Center for Health Statistics, *Health Statistics on Older Persons,* 1986: 7, 11.

111. Data are for 1987. National Center for Health Statistics, *Health: United States 1988,* 1989: 78.

112. Data are for 1987. National Center for Health Statistics, *Health: United States 1988,* 1989: 78.

113. Data are for 1987. National Center for Health Statistics, *Health: United States 1988,* 1989: 78.

114. *Mature Market Report,* April 1989: 1.

115. *Mature Market Report,* April 1989: 1.

116. *Mature Market Report,* April 1989: 1.

117. *Mature Market Report,* April 1989: 1.

118. *Mature Market Report,* April 1989: 1.

119. *Senior Edition USA,* October 1989: 25.

120. *Senior Edition USA,* October 1989: 25.

121. *Senior Edition USA,* October 1989: 25.

122. National Institute on Aging, *Answers about Aging,* Butler, 1988: 2.

123. National Institute on Aging, *Special Report,* 1988: 13.

124. Based on National Center for Health Statistics, *Health: United States 1988,* 1989: 74.

125. Data are for 1986. National Center for Health Statistics, *Health: United States 1988,* 1989: 74.

126. Data are for 1986. National Center for Health Statistics, *Health: United States 1988,* 1989: 74.

127. Data are for 1986. National Center for Health Statistics, *Health: United States 1988,* 1989: 74.

128. Data are for 1986. National Center for Health Statistics, *Health: United States 1988,* 1989: 74.

129. Data are for 1986. Nevada has a rate of 47 suicides per 100,000 people age 75 to 79 compared to 21 nationally in 1987. *Older Americans Reports,* September 15, 1989: 359.

130. National Center for Health Statistics, *Health: United States 1988,* 1989: 74.

131. Data are for 1986. National Center for Health Statistics, *Health: United States 1988,* 1989: 74.

132. Data are for 1986. National Center for Health Statistics, *Health: United States 1988,* 1989: 74.

133. Data are for 1986. National Center for Health Statistics, *Health: United States 1988,* 1989: 74.

134. Data are for 1986. National Center for Health Statistics, *Health: United States 1988,* 1989: 74.

135. Data are for 1986. National Center for Health Statistics, *Health: United States 1988,* 1989: 74.

136. Data are for 1982–87. National Center for Health Statistics, *Health: United States 1988,* 1989: 94.

137. Data are for 1988. National Center for Health Statistics, *Current Estimates 1988,* 1989: 27.

138. National Center for Health Statistics, *Current Estimates 1988,* 1989: 16.

139. Data are for 1987. National Center for Health Statistics, *Health: United States 1988,* 1989: 94.

140. Data are for 1987. National Center for Health Statistics, *Health: United States 1988,* 1989: 94.

141. U.S. Senate Special Committee on Aging, *Aging America,* 1987: 97.

142. National Center for Health Statistics, *Current Estimates 1988,* 1989: 84–85.

143. Study by Kenneth Manton, Duke University, Reported in U.S. Senate Special Committee on Aging, *Developments in Aging 1987,* 1988: 9.

144. National Center for Health Statistics, *Current Estimates 1988,* 1989: 85.

145. Data are for 1988. National Center for Health Statistics, *Current Estimates 1988,* 1989: 86.

146. Data are for 1988. National Center for Health Statistics, *Current Estimates 1988,* 1989: 87.

147. National Center for Health Statistics, *Current Estimates 1988,* 1989: 84.

148. National Center for Health Statistics, *Current Estimates 1988,* 1989: 84.

149. Data are for 1988. National Center for Health Statistics, *Current Estimates 1988,* 1989: 84.

150. Data are for 1988. National Center for Health Statistics, *Current Estimates 1988,* 1989: 84.

151. National Institute on Aging, *Special Report,* 1988: 13.

152. National Institute on Aging, *The Aging Woman,* undated: 20.

153. Data are for 1988. National Center for Health Statistics, *Current Estimates 1988,* 1989: 85.

154. National Institute on Aging, *The Aging Woman,* undated, 16.

155. National Institute on Aging, *Answers about Aging,* Riggs, 1988: 1.

156. U.S. Department of Health and Human Services, *Surgeon General's Workshop,* 1988: G-4.

157. National Institute on Aging, *Answers about Aging,* Riggs, 1988: 1.

158. National Institute on Aging, *Answers about Aging,* Riggs, 1988: 1.

159. National Institute on Aging, *Answers about Aging,* Riggs, 1988: 1.

160. National Institute on Aging, *Answers about Aging,* Riggs, 1988: 1.

161. National Institute on Aging, *Answers about Aging,* Riggs, 1988: 1.

162. National Institute on Aging, *Answers about Aging,* Riggs, 1988: 1.

163. National Institute on Aging, *Answers about Aging,* Riggs, 1988: 3.

164. National Institute on Aging, *Answers about Aging,* Riggs, 1988: 3.

165. Based on data from the National Center for Health Statistics, *Current Estimates 1988,* 1989: 72.

166. Data are for 1988. National Center for Health Statistics, *Current Estimates 1988,* 1989: 72.

167. U.S Bureau of the Census, *Statistical Abstract 1988,* 1987: 105.

168. U.S Bureau of the Census, *Statistical Abstract 1988,* 1987: 105.

169. National Center for Health Statistics, *Current Estimates 1988,* 1989: 74.

170. National Center for Health Statistics, *Current Estimates 1988,* 1989: 72.

171. National Center for Health Statistics, *Current Estimates 1988,* 1989: 74.

172. Data are for 1986. National Center for Health Statistics, *Health: United States 1988,* 1989: 72.

173. Data are for 1986. National Center for Health Statistics, *Health: United States 1988,* 1989: 72.

174. Data are for 1986. National Center for Health Statistics, *Health: United States 1988,* 1989: 72.

175. U.S. Department of Health and Human Services, *Databook on the Elderly,* 1987: 50.

176. U.S. Department of Health and Human Services, *Surgeon General's Workshop,* 1988: D-1.

177. U.S. Department of Health and Human Services, *Surgeon General's Workshop,* 1988: D-1.

178. U.S. Department of Health and Human Services, *Surgeon General's Workshop,* 1988: D-1.

179. U.S. Department of Health and Human Services, *Surgeon General's Workshop,* 1988: A-10.

180. U.S. Department of Health and Human Services, *Surgeon General's Workshop,* 1988: D-1.

181. U.S. Department of Health and Human Services, *Surgeon General's Workshop,* 1988: D-1.

182. U.S. Department of Health and Human Services, *Surgeon General's Workshop,* 1988: D-1.

183. U.S. Department of Health and Human Services, *Surgeon General's Workshop,* 1988: D-1.

184. U.S. Department of Health and Human Services, *Surgeon General's Workshop,* 1988: D-1.

185. U.S. Department of Health and Human Services, *Surgeon General's Workshop,* 1988: D-1.

186. U.S. Department of Health and Human Services, *Surgeon General's Workshop,* 1988: D-1.

187. Veterans Administration study. Reported in *Mature Market Report,* June/July 1989: 6.

188. Data are from the National Survey of Oral Health, 1985–86. Reported in *Mature Market Report,* January 1989: 11.

189. Data are for 1983, the latest data available. U.S. Department of Health and Human Services, *Surgeon General's Workshop,* 1988: B2.

190. Data are for 1983, the latest data available. U.S. Department of Health and Human Services, *Surgeon General's Workshop,* 1988: B3.

191. Data are for 1981, the latest data available. U.S. Department of Health and Human Services, *Surgeon General's Workshop,* 1988: B3.

192. Data are for 1981, the latest data available. U.S. Department of Health and Human Services, *Surgeon General's Workshop,* 1988: B3.

193. Data are for 1986. National Center for Health Statistics, *Use of Dental Services,* 1988: 17.

194. Data are for 1986. National Center for Health Statistics, *Use of Dental Services,* 1988: 17.

195. Based on 1986 data. National Center for Health Statistics, *Health: United States 1988,* 1989: 110.
196. U.S. Bureau of the Census, *Statistical Abstract 1988,* 1987: 110.
197. U.S. Bureau of the Census, *Statistical Abstract 1988,* 1987: 110.
198. U.S. Bureau of the Census, *Statistical Abstract 1988,* 1987: 110.
199. U.S. Bureau of the Census, *Statistical Abstract 1988,* 1987: 110.
200. U.S. Bureau of the Census, *Statistical Abstract 1988,* 1987: 110.
201. U.S. Bureau of the Census, *Statistical Abstract 1988,* 1987: 110.
202. U.S. Bureau of the Census, *Statistical Abstract 1988,* 1987: 110.
203. U.S. Bureau of the Census, *Statistical Abstract 1988,* 1987: 110.
204. U.S. Bureau of the Census, *Statistical Abstract 1988,* 1987: 110.
205. National Institute on Aging, *The Aging Man,* undated: 20.
206. National Institute on Aging, *The Aging Man,* undated: 21.
207. National Institute on Aging, *The Aging Man,* undated: 19.
208. U.S. Bureau of the Census, *Statistical Abstract 1988,* 1987: 110.
209. U.S. Bureau of the Census, *Statistical Abstract 1988,* 1987: 110.
210. U.S. Bureau of the Census, *Statistical Abstract 1988,* 1987: 110.
211. U.S. Bureau of the Census, *Statistical Abstract 1988,* 1987: 110.
212. U.S. Bureau of the Census, *Statistical Abstract 1988,* 1987: 110.
213. U.S. Bureau of the Census, *Statistical Abstract 1988,* 1987: 110.
214. National Institute on Aging, *The Aging Man,* undated: 22.
215. National Institute on Aging, *The Aging Man,* undated: 22.
216. National Institute on Aging, *Special Report,* 1988: 3.
217. National Institute on Aging, *The Aging Man,* undated: 22.
218. National Institute on Aging, *The Aging Woman,* undated: 11.
219. National Institute on Aging, *The Aging Woman,* undated: 11.
220. National Institute on Aging, *The Aging Woman,* undated: 11.
221. National Institute on Aging, *The Aging Woman,* undated: 11.
222. National Institute on Aging, *The Aging Man,* undated: 15.
223. National Institute on Aging, *Special Report,* 1988: 18.
224. National Center for Health Statistics, *Current Estimates 1988,* 1989: 85.
225. National Institute on Aging, *Special Report,* 1988: 35.
226. National Center for Health Statistics, *Current Estimates 1988,* 1989: 84.
227. National Center for Health Statistics, *Current Estimates 1988,* 1989: 85.
228. U.S. Senate Special Committee on Aging, *Aging America,* 1987: 101.
229. U.S. Senate Special Committee on Aging, *Aging America,* 1987: 101.
230. U.S. Senate Special Committee on Aging, *Aging America,* 1987: 101.
231. National Institute on Aging, "News Notes," November 9, 1989. Findings were also published in: D. A. Evans, H. H. Funkenstein, and M. S. Albert, "Clinically-Diagnosed Alzheimer's Disease: An Epidemiological Study in a Community Population of Older Persons," *Journal of the American Medical Association,* November 10, 1989.
232. National Institute on Aging, "News Notes," November 9, 1989.
233. National Institute on Aging, "News Notes," November 9, 1989.
234. National Institute on Aging, "News Notes," November 9, 1989.
235. National Institute on Aging, "News Notes," November 9, 1989.
236. National Institute on Aging, "News Notes," November 9, 1989.
237. *Older Americans Reports,* April 1, 1989: 138.
238. U.S. Senate Special Committee on Aging, *Aging America,* 1987: 119.

239. U.S. Senate Special Committee on Aging, *Aging America,* 1987: 119.

240. U.S. Department of Health and Human Services, *Surgeon General's Workshop,* 1988: F-5.

241. U.S. Department of Health and Human Services, *Surgeon General's Workshop,* 1988: F-6.

242. Harris, 1986: 45.

243. Walz, 1986: 623.

244. *Older Americans Reports,* April 15, 1989: 158.

245. Includes major depression, dysthmia, cyclothymic disorder, dysphorias, and atypical depression. U.S. Department of Health and Human Services, *Surgeon General's Workshop,* 1988: F-6.

246. U.S. Department of Health and Human Services, *Surgeon General's Workshop,* 1988: F-6.

247. National Institute on Aging, *The Aging Woman,* undated: 11.

248. Harris, 1986: 44.

249. Harris, 1986: 43.

250. U.S. Department of Health and Human Services, *Surgeon General's Workshop,* 1988: F-7.

251. U.S. Department of Health and Human Services, *Surgeon General's Workshop,* 1988: F-7.

252. American Association of Homes for the Aging, *Provider News,* 1989: 4.

253. American Association of Homes for the Aging, *Provider News,* 1989: 4.

254. Brody, 1988: B6. U.S. Department of Health and Human Services, *Surgeon General's Workshop,* 1988: A-4.

255. Data are for 1984. U.S. Department of Health and Human Services, *Databook on the Elderly,* 1987: 53.

256. U.S. Department of Health and Human Services, *Surgeon General's Workshop,* 1988: A-4.

257. U.S. Department of Health and Human Services, *Surgeon General's Workshop,* 1988: E-3.

258. *Older Americans Reports,* December 15, 1989: 484.

259. U.S. Department of Health and Human Services, *Surgeon General's Workshop,* 1988: G-3.

260. U.S. Department of Health and Human Services, *Surgeon General's Workshop,* 1988: G-3.

261. U.S. Department of Health and Human Services, *Surgeon General's Workshop,* 1988: G-3.

262. Study by Dr. Pearl German at Johns Hopkins University. Reported in National Institute on Aging, *Special Report,* 1988: 12.

263. Study by Dr. Pearl German at Johns Hopkins University. Reported in National Institute on Aging, *Special Report,* 1988: 12.

264. *Older Americans Reports,* December 15, 1989: 484.

265. Study by Dr. Pearl German at Johns Hopkins University. Reported in National Institute on Aging, *Special Report,* 1988: 13.

266. Study by Dr. Pearl German at Johns Hopkins University. Reported in National Institute on Aging, *Special Report,* 1988: 13.

267. Testimony in front of the U.S. House of Representatives Select Committee on Aging by Frank Young, then commissioner of the Food and Drug Administration. April 19, 1989.

268. Testimony in front of the U.S. House of Representatives Select Committee on Aging by Frank Young, then commissioner of the Food and Drug Administration. April 19, 1989.
269. Testimony in front of the U.S. House of Representatives Select Committee on Aging by Frank Young, then commissioner of the Food and Drug Administration. April 19, 1989.
270. *Mature Market Report,* August/September 1989: 7.
271. Study by Dr. Pearl German at Johns Hopkins University. Reported in National Institute on Aging, *Special Report,* 1988: 13.
272. Study by Dr. Pearl German at Johns Hopkins University. Reported in National Institute on Aging, *Special Report,* 1988: 13.

Chapter 14

Use of Health Services

Hospitalization

More than One-Third of Seniors Hospitalized Each Year

Every day in the United States: 31,991 seniors are discharged from hospitals.[1]

Percentage of all hospital discharges that are to seniors: 31.[2]

Percentage of seniors who are hospitalized in a year: 37.[3]

Percentage of all short-stay hospital days of care that are by seniors: 42.[4] (Short-stay hospitals are those in which the average length of stay is less than 30 days.)

Diseases of the circulatory system as a portion of all "first-listed" diagnoses for senior hospital patients: about one-third.[5]
(First-listed diagnosis is the diagnosis listed first on the hospital's medical record for the patient.)

The number of diagnoses per discharge of senior patients compared to younger patients: about four versus two.[6]

Length of Hospital Stays

Average length of hospital stays for seniors: 9 days.[7]

The decline in the average length of a hospital stay between 1983 and 1985: one full day.[8]

The decline since 1985: minimal.[9]

The average length of stay for persons age 65 to 74: 8 days.[10]

The average stay for persons over age 75: 9 days.[11]

Older Men Most Likely To Face Surgery

The rate of men over the age of 65 undergoing an operation compared to the rate for men of all ages: the rate for men over age 65 is three times higher.[12]

The rate of having operations for men over 65 compared to men of all ages: 255.5 per 1,000 versus 76.4 per 1,000.[13]

The rate for women over 65 compared to women of all ages: 187.9 per 1,000 versus 118.3 per 1,000.[14]

Using Physician Services

Most Seniors Get Regular Care

Portion of seniors with a regular source of medical care: 9 in 10.[15]

Percentage of persons over age 50 who say they go for regular health check-ups: 45.[16]

Percentage of seniors who report that they sometimes go without medical help when they think they need it: 13.[17]

Physician Contacts Frequent among Seniors

Every day in the United States: 778,000 seniors contact a physician about a medical problem.[18]

Percentage of all physician contacts that are made by seniors: 15.[19]

Number of physician contacts the average senior makes in a year: 9.[20]

Percentage of seniors who have contacted a physician within the last year: 85.[21]

Portion of seniors who have not contacted a physician in two years or more: 1 in 10.[22]

Portion of physician contacts by seniors that are made by telephone: 1 in 8.[23]

Portion made at the doctor's office: almost 2 in 3.[24]

Portion made in a hospital: 1 in 8.[25]

Older People More Likely To Contact Physicians

Average number of annual contacts with physicians for persons age 45 to 64: 6.[26]

For persons age 65 to 74: 8.[27]

For persons age 75 and over: 9.[28]

Those Living Alone More Likely To Visit Doctors, Spend Less Time in Bed

The number of times per year seniors living alone visit doctors compared with those living with others: 7 versus 4.5.[29]

The average number of days seniors living alone spend in bed compared with those living with others: 11 versus 19.[30]

Demand for Physician Services Expected To Increase

By the year 2000 demand for physician services by seniors will increase by 22 percent from 250 million to 304 million contacts.[31]

By the year 2030 demand will increase by 129 percent to more than 570 million contacts.[32]

Notes

1. Based on National Center for Health Statistics, *Utilization of Short-Stay Hospitals,* 1988: 21.
2. National Center for Health Statistics, *Utilization of Short-Stay Hospitals,* 1988: 21.
3. National Center for Health Statistics, *Utilization of Short-Stay Hospitals,* 1988: 21.
4. National Center for Health Statistics, *Utilization of Short-Stay Hospitals,* 1988: 21.
5. National Center for Health Statistics, *Utilization of Short-Stay Hospitals,* 1988: 30.
6. U.S. Senate Special Committee on Aging, *Aging America,* 1987: 114.
7. National Center for Health Statistics, *Utilization of Short-Stay Hospitals,* 1988: 21.
8. National Center for Health Statistics, *Utilization of Short-Stay Hospitals,* 1988: 2.
9. National Center for Health Statistics, *Utilization of Short-Stay Hospitals,* 1988: 2.
10. National Center for Health Statistics, *Utilization of Short-Stay Hospitals,* 1988: 21.

11. National Center for Health Statistics, *Utilization of Short-Stay Hospitals,* 1988: 21.
12. National Center for Health Statistics, *Health: United States 1988,* 1989: 118.
13. National Center for Health Statistics, *Health: United States 1988,* 1989: 118.
14. National Center for Health Statistics, *Health: United States 1988,* 1989: 118.
15. U.S. Department of Health and Human Services, *Databook on the Elderly,* 1987: 58–60.
16. Daniel Yankelovich Group, 1987: 11.
17. Harris, 1986: 44.
18. Based on National Center for Health Statistics, *Current Estimates 1988,* 1989, 117.
19. A contact with a physician may be made by telephone, in an office or hospital, or by other means. National Center for Health Statistics, *Current Estimates 1988,* 1989: 117.
20. A contact with a physician may be made by telephone, in an office or hospital, or by other means. National Center for Health Statistics, *Current Estimates 1988,* 1989: 117.
21. A contact with a physician may be made by telephone, in an office or hospital, or by other means. National Center for Health Statistics, *Current Estimates 1988,* 1989: 118.
22. A contact with a physician may be made by telephone, in an office or hospital, or by other means. National Center for Health Statistics, *Current Estimates 1988,* 1989: 118.
23. A contact with a physician may be made by telephone, in an office or hospital, or by other means. National Center for Health Statistics, *Current Estimates 1988,* 1989: 117.
24. A contact with a physician may be made by telephone, in an office or hospital, or by other means. National Center for Health Statistics, *Current Estimates 1988,* 1989: 117.
25. A contact with a physician may be made by telephone, in an office or hospital, or by other means. National Center for Health Statistics, *Current Estimates 1988,* 1989: 117.
26. A contact with a physician may be made by telephone, in an office or hospital, or by other means. National Center for Health Statistics, *Current Estimates 1988,* 1989: 116.
27. A contact with a physician may be made by telephone, in an office or hospital, or by other means. National Center for Health Statistics, *Current Estimates 1988,* 1989: 116.
28. A contact with a physician may be made by telephone, in an office or hospital, or by other means. National Center for Health Statistics, *Current Estimates 1988,* 1989: 116.
29. *Older Americans Reports,* April 15, 1988: 158.
30. *Older Americans Reports,* April 15, 1988: 158.
31. Projections by Donald Fowles, U.S. Administration on Aging. Reported in U.S. Senate Special Committee on Aging, *Aging America,* 1989: 95.
32. Projections by Donald Fowles, U.S. Administration on Aging. Reported in U.S. Senate Special Committee on Aging, *Aging America,* 1989: 95.

Chapter 15

Long-Term Care

Who Needs Long-Term Care?

Long-Term Care Needs Are Increasing

Portion of seniors living in the community who require some form of help for a limitation: about one-quarter (23 percent).[1] (Limitations include difficulty with walking, bathing, getting outside the house, transferring from a bed or chair, dressing, getting to or using a toilet, or eating. These are commonly called limitations in activities of daily living [ADLs].)

The percentage of families who have experienced a long-term care problem within the family: 47.[2]

The number of seniors in need of long-term care in 1989: 7.1 million.[3]

The number who will need long-term care by 2000: 8.9 million.[4]

The number in need by 2020: 12.3 million.[5]

Oldest Seniors More Likely To Need Long-Term Care

Percentage of persons 65 to 74 who require some form of help for a limitation: 17.[6]

Of persons 75 to 84: 28.[7]

Of persons 85 and over: 49.[8]

Many Who Need Help Don't Get It

The number of community residents over age 70 with limitations in activities of daily living (ADLs) in 1986: 4.5 million.[9]

Of these the portion who receive no help: well over half.[10]

Portion of those who receive help that is unpaid (most often by family members): almost a third.[11]

The portion of long-term care recipients who rely on paid help: 6 percent.[12]

Poor Least Likely To Get Help

The number of community residents over age 70 with limitations in daily activity who had incomes below the poverty level in 1986: 1 million.[13]

The portion of these who received no help: almost two-thirds.[14]

Long-Term Care in the Community

Most Recipients Cared for at Home

The portion of long-term care recipients who receive services at home: 4 in 5.[15]

The portion who receive services in nursing homes: 1 in 5.[16]

Most Informal Caregivers Are Married Women

The number of family members providing long-term care to parents or others: 9 to 10 million.[17]

Portion of "informal" caregivers that are women: three-quarters.[18] (Informal caregivers do not receive pay for their services. They are usually family members.)

The mean age of caregivers: 57.[19]

Portion of caregivers who also hold down jobs: almost one-third.[20]

Portion who are married: 7 in 10.[21]

Portion who live with the person for whom they are providing care: three-quarters.[22]

Wives, Adult Children Provide Care

The primary caregiver for men: a wife.[23]

The primary caregiver for women: adult children.[24]

The number of years that women will spend caring for their parents versus caring for their children: 18 years versus 17 years.[25]

The number of women who are caring for both children and parents simultaneously: 2 million.[26]

Caregivers Who Work

According to surveys the portion of workers who provide care to seniors: 1 to 2 in 5.[27]

According to a survey of corporate executives the percentage who say that they have been personally responsible for the care of a senior in the last two years: 49.[28]

The portion of caregiving workers who report that they work less effectively because of worry about the older person: 7 in 10.[29]

Types of Help Provided by Informal Caregivers

Percentage of caregivers providing shopping and transportation help to seniors: 86.[30]

Percentage providing help with household tasks: 81.[31]

Percentage providing help with personal hygiene: 67.[32]

Percentage providing help with administration of medicines: 53.[33]

Percentage providing help with handling finances: 49.[34]

Percentage providing help with mobility: 46.[35]

Percentage of seniors with 3 or more functional limitations who use visiting nurse/home health aide services: 50.[36]

Nursing Home Stays

Nursing Home Residents a Minority

Percentage of seniors who are in nursing homes at any given time: 5.[37]

In 1985 the estimated number of seniors living in nursing homes: 1.3 million.[38]

Percentage of nursing home beds that were occupied by seniors in 1985: 88.[39]

The Chance of Entering a Nursing Home Increases with Age

The chance of entering a nursing home for persons age 65 to 74: 1 in 100.[40]

The chance for persons age 75 to 84: 3 in 50.[41]

The chance for persons 85 and over: 1 in 5.[42]

Risk of Institutionalization

The chance that sometime during an individual's life he or she will spend at least some time in a nursing home: 1 in 2.[43]

The chance of spending a year or more in a nursing home: 1 in 4.[44]

The average nursing home resident: an 80-year-old white widow with several chronic conditions who was admitted from a hospital. She will stay under one year.[45]

The risk factors that increase the chances for institutionalization:

• High level of chronic disability

• Deteriorating cognitive functioning

• Advancing age

• Being female

• Spending time in a hospital or other health facility.[46]

Percentage of seniors who say that the fear of being confined to an institution is a major worry for them: 13.[47]

Most Nursing Home Residents Are Women

The portion of nursing home residents who are women: 3 in 4.[48]

The likelihood that an older woman will enter a nursing home compared to an older man: twice as likely.[49]

The portion of women over age 85 who are in nursing homes: 1 in 4.[50]

The portion of men this age: 1 in 7.[51]

Most Nursing Home Residents Are White

Percentage of nursing home residents who are white: 93.[52]

Percentage who are black: 6.[53]

Percentage who are Asian, Pacific Islander, American Indian, or Alaska natives: less than one.[54]

Most Nursing Home Residents Are Not Married

Portion of nursing home residents who are married: 1 in 6.[55]

Compared to the noninstitutionalized elderly: 1 in 2.[56]

Portion of older nursing home residents who have children: 3 in 5.[57]

Compared to older people in the community: 4 in 5.[58]

Cognitive Impairments, Incontinence Common among Residents

Portion of nursing home residents with bowel or urinary incontinence: over half.[59]

Portion with disorientation or memory impairment: almost two-thirds.[60]

Portion with senile dementia or chronic organic brain syndrome: almost half.[61]

Percentage of nursing home residents who require assistance with bathing: 91.[62]

Most Residents Admitted from Health Care Facilities

Percentage of nursing home residents admitted from a private or semi-private residence: 28.[63]

Percentage admitted from a health care facility: 69.[64]

Length of Stay

Every day in the United States: 355 seniors are discharged from nursing homes.[65]

The percentage of nursing home residents who are discharged alive: 72.[66]

The percentage of nursing home residents who are discharged alive who stay less than a year: 79.[67]

The percentage who stay less than a month: 32.[68]

The percentage who are discharged to other health care facilities: 68.[69]

The percentage who return home: about 30.[70]

The average number of days men over age 85 spend in a nursing home the year before their death: 111.[71]

The average number of days for women over age 85: 173.[72]

Nursing Home Residents Expected To Increase

The number of Americans expected to be residents of nursing homes in 2000: 2 million.[73]

The number in 2040: 4.6 million.[74]

Costs of Nursing Homes

Percentage of persons 45 to 54 who say they do not know what the costs of nursing homes might be: 24.[75]

Percentage of persons over age 65: 28.[76]

Portion of both age groups who significantly underestimate the average costs of nursing home care: almost half.[77]

Percentage of Maine residents who think Medicare will help pay for long-term care: 85.[78] (Medicare does *not* pay for long-term care.)

The annual cost of nursing home care for the cognitively impaired: $22,300.[79]

Nursing home average monthly charges in 1985 for Medicare beneficiaries: $2,141.[80]

For Medicaid recipients: $1,504.[81]

For public assistance recipients: $863.[82]

For all other sources: $1,099.[83]

Portion of nursing home residents who pay for their nursing home care out of their own pockets at admission: half.[84]

Percentage whose first month or more is covered by Medicare: 5.[85]

Percentage whose stay is covered by Medicaid: 40.[86]

Psychological Abuse in Nursing Homes

In a survey of 577 nurses and nurses' aides in long-term care facilities, the portion who had seen at least one incident of psychological abuse of a resident in the preceding year: 4 in 5.[87]

The portion who reported that they themselves had committed psychologically abusive acts: 2 in 5.[88]

The most prevalent form of psychological abuse observed by respondents: yelling at a patient in anger, with over two-thirds of the survey respondents having observed at least one such incident.[89]

The second most common form of psychological abuse: insulting or swearing at a patient, with half of the respondents having seen such abuse in the previous year.[90]

Percentage of respondents who reported that they had seen patients isolated inappropriately: 23.[91]

Percentage who had seen residents threatened: 15.[92]

Percentage who had seen patients denied food or privileges: 13.[93]

Physical Abuse in Nursing Homes

In a survey of 577 nurses and nurses' aides in long-term care facilities, the portion who had seen at least one incident of physical abuse of a resident in the preceding year: over one-third.[94]

The portion who reported that they themselves had committed one or more physically abusive acts: 1 in 10.[95]

The most prevalent form of physical abuse observed: physical restraint, with more than 1 in 5 survey respondents having observed at least one such incident.[96]

Of those who had witnessed physical restraint of residents, the portion who had seen it on multiple occasions: two-thirds.[97]

The second most common form of physical abuse observed: pushing, grabbing, shoving, or pinching a patient, with 1 in 6 respondents having seen such abuse in the previous year.[98]

Of those who had witnessed this form of abuse, the portion who had seen it on multiple occasions: 3 in 5.[99]

The percentage of respondents who had seen slapping or hitting of residents: 12.[100]

Need for Nursing Home Workers Increasing

The number of nursing aides and home health aides currently providing long-term care services: 1.5 million.[101]

By the year 2000 the number of additional workers that will be needed to take care of those in need of long-term care: 500,000.[102]

The Cost of Long-Term Care

Most Americans Believe They Cannot Afford Care

The percentage of Americans who believe that they cannot afford to pay for the cost of long-term care: 82.[103]

Percentage of Americans with incomes over $50,000 who believe that they cannot afford to pay for the cost of long-term care: 61.[104]

Percentage of Americans with incomes of $7,500 or less who believe that they cannot afford to pay for the cost of long-term care: 93.[105]

Most Americans Will Use Savings, Assets To Pay for Care

The financial sources that the majority of Americans say they will use to pay for long-term care: savings and assets.[106]

The percentage of seniors who say they will use home equity to pay for long-term care: 21.[107]

How Much It Costs

The annual cost of care in the community for the cognitively impaired: $11,700 versus $22,300 for nursing home care.[108]

Average charge of a Medicare home health care visit in 1990: $73.[109]

The amount U.S. consumers spent on in-home care in 1986: $14 billion.[110]

The amount that the government estimates consumers will spend for in-home care by 2000: $60 billion.[111]

Example of the savings home care can represent: the average cost for a ventilator-dependent patient in a hospital is $270, 830 per year compared to $21,192 per year for in-home care.[112]

Notes

1. Based on limitations in activities of daily living such as walking, bathing, getting outside the house, transferring from a bed or chair, dressing, getting to and using the toilet, and eating. American Association of Retired Persons (AARP), *Changing Needs,* undated: 28–29.
2. Survey by the American Association of Retired Persons (AARP) and the Villers Foundation. Reported in American Association of Retired Persons (AARP), *Changing Needs,* undated: 116.
3. The Long-Term Care Campaign, "What Is Long-Term Care?" 1989: 1.
4. The Long-Term Care Campaign, "What Is Long-Term Care?" 1989: 2.
5. The Long-Term Care Campaign, "What Is Long-Term Care?" 1989: 2.
6. Based on limitations in activities of daily living such as walking, bathing, getting outside the house, transferring from a bed or chair, dressing, getting to and using the toilet, and eating. American Association of Retired Persons (AARP), *Changing Needs,* undated: 28–29.
7. Based on limitations in activities of daily living such as walking, bathing, getting outside the house, transferring from a bed or chair, dressing, getting to and using the toilet, and eating. American Association of Retired Persons (AARP), *Changing Needs,* undated: 28–29.
8. Based on limitations in activities of daily living such as walking, bathing, getting outside the house, transferring from a bed or chair, dressing, getting to and using the toilet, and eating. American Association of Retired Persons (AARP), *Changing Needs,* undated: 28–29.
9. American Association of Retired Persons (AARP), *Changing Needs,* undated: 44.
10. American Association of Retired Persons (AARP), *Changing Needs,* undated: 44.
11. American Association of Retired Persons (AARP), *Changing Needs,* undated: 44.
12. American Association of Retired Persons (AARP), *Changing Needs,* undated: 44.
13. American Association of Retired Persons (AARP), *Changing Needs,* undated: 44.
14. American Association of Retired Persons (AARP), *Changing Needs,* undated: 44.
15. U.S. Senate Special Committee on Aging, *Developments in Aging 1987,* 1988: 10.
16. U.S. Senate Special Committee on Aging, *Developments in Aging 1987,* 1988: 10.
17. The Long-Term Care Campaign, *Facts about Caregivers,* 1989: 1.
18. Data are from the 1982 Long-Term Care Survey and were prepared by Robin Stone, National Center for Health Services Research. Reported in U.S. Senate Special Committee on Aging, *Developments in Aging 1987,* 1988: 21.
19. Data are from the 1982 Long-Term Care Survey and were prepared by Robin Stone, National Center for Health Services Research. Reported in U.S. Senate Special Committee on Aging, *Developments in Aging 1987,* 1988: 21.
20. Data are from the 1982 Long-Term Care Survey and were prepared by Robin Stone, National Center for Health Services Research. Reported in U.S. Senate Special Committee on Aging, *Developments in Aging 1987,* 1988: 22.
21. Data are from the 1982 Long-Term Care Survey and were prepared by Robin Stone, National Center for Health Services Research. Reported in U.S. Senate Special Committee on Aging, *Developments in Aging 1987,* 1988: 22.
22. Data are from the 1982 Long-Term Care Survey and were prepared by Robin Stone, National Center for Health Services Research. Reported in U.S. Senate Special Committee on Aging, *Developments in Aging 1987,* 1988: 22.

23. Data are from the 1982 Long-Term Care Survey and were prepared by Robin Stone, National Center for Health Services Research. Reported in U.S. Senate Special Committee on Aging, *Developments in Aging 1987,* 1988: 20.

24. Data are from the 1982 Long-Term Care Survey and were prepared by Robin Stone, National Center for Health Services Research. Reported in U.S. Senate Special Committee on Aging, *Developments in Aging 1987,* 1988: 20.

25. Study by the Older Women's League (OWL). Reported in *Older Americans Reports,* May 12, 1989: 189.

26. Study by the Older Women's League (OWL). Reported in *Older Americans Reports,* May 12, 1989: 189.

27. *Older Americans Reports,* November 3, 1989: 425. *Mature Market Report,* June/July 1989: 3.

28. *Mature Market Report,* June/July 1989: 3.

29. *Older Americans Reports,* November 3, 1989: 425.

30. American Association of Retired Persons (AARP), *Changing Needs,* undated: 51.

31. American Association of Retired Persons (AARP), *Changing Needs,* undated: 51.

32. American Association of Retired Persons (AARP), *Changing Needs,* undated: 51.

33. American Association of Retired Persons (AARP), *Changing Needs,* undated: 51.

34. American Association of Retired Persons (AARP), *Changing Needs,* undated: 51.

35. American Association of Retired Persons (AARP), *Changing Needs,* undated: 51.

36. American Association of Retired Persons (AARP), *Changing Needs,* undated: 68.

37. National Center for Health Statistics, *Use of Nursing Homes,* 1987: 1.

38. National Center for Health Statistics, *Use of Nursing Homes,* 1987: 2.

39. National Center for Health Statistics, *Use of Nursing Homes,* 1987: 2.

40. National Center for Health Statistics, *Use of Nursing Homes,* 1987: 2.

41. National Center for Health Statistics, *Use of Nursing Homes,* 1987: 2.

42. National Center for Health Statistics, *Use of Nursing Homes,* 1987: 2.

43. The Long-Term Care Campaign, "What Is Long-Term Care?" 1989: 2.

44. The Long-Term Care Campaign, "What Is Long-Term Care?" 1989: 2.

45. American Association of Retired Persons (AARP), *Changing Needs,* undated: 71, 80.

46. American Association of Retired Persons (AARP), *Changing Needs,* undated: 71.

47. Harris, 1986: 45.

48. National Center for Health Statistics, *Use of Nursing Homes,* 1987: 2.

49. American Association of Retired Persons (AARP), *Changing Needs,* undated: 72.

50. National Center for Health Statistics, *Use of Nursing Homes,* 1987: 2.

51. National Center for Health Statistics, *Use of Nursing Homes,* 1987: 2.

52. National Center for Health Statistics, *Use of Nursing Homes,* 1987: 2.

53. National Center for Health Statistics, *Use of Nursing Homes,* 1987: 2.

54. National Center for Health Statistics, *Use of Nursing Homes,* 1987: 2.

55. National Center for Health Statistics, *Use of Nursing Homes,* 1987: 6.

56. U.S. Senate Special Committee on Aging, *Aging America,* 1989: 108.

57. National Center for Health Statistics, *Use of Nursing Homes,* 1987: 7.

58. U.S. Senate Special Committee on Aging, *Developments in Aging 1987,* 1988: 16.

59. National Center for Health Statistics, *Use of Nursing Homes,* 1987: 5.

60. National Center for Health Statistics, *Use of Nursing Homes,* 1987: 6.

61. National Center for Health Statistics, *Use of Nursing Homes,* 1987: 6.

62. National Center for Health Statistics, *Use of Nursing Homes,* 1987: 6.

63. National Center for Health Statistics, *Discharges,* 1987: 3.

64. National Center for Health Statistics, *Discharges,* 1987: 3.
65. Based on National Center for Health Statistics, *Use of Nursing Homes,* 1987.
66. National Center for Health Statistics, *Discharges,* 1987: 7.
67. National Center for Health Statistics, *Discharges,* 1987: 9.
68. National Center for Health Statistics, *Discharges,* 1987: 9.
69. National Center for Health Statistics, *Discharges,* 1987: 4.
70. National Center for Health Statistics, *Discharges,* 1987: 4.
71. *Mature Market Report,* March 1988: 10.
72. *Mature Market Report,* March 1988: 10.
73. Projections by Donald Fowles, Administration on Aging. Reported in U.S. Senate Special Committee on Aging, *Aging America,* 1989: 98.
74. Projections by Donald Fowles, Administration on Aging. Reported in U.S. Senate Special Committee on Aging, *Aging America,* 1989: 98.
75. Survey of 1,000 adults conducted by New World Decisions for Transamerica Life Companies. Transamerica Life Companies, 1988: 2.
76. Survey of 1,000 adults conducted by New World Decisions for Transamerica Life Companies. Transamerica Life Companies, 1988: 2.
77. Survey of 1,000 adults conducted by New World Decisions for Transamerica Life Companies. Transamerica Life Companies, 1988: 2.
78. *Older Americans Reports,* October 28, 1988: 424.
79. Coughlin, 1989: 173.
80. National Center for Health Statistics, *Health: United States 1988,* 1989: 162.
81. National Center for Health Statistics, *Health: United States 1988,* 1989: 162.
82. National Center for Health Statistics, *Health: United States 1988,* 1989: 162.
83. National Center for Health Statistics, *Health: United States 1988,* 1989: 162.
84. Based on the 1985 National Nursing Home Survey. National Center for Health Statistics, *Use of Nursing Homes,* 1987: 9.
85. Based on the 1985 National Nursing Home Survey. National Center for Health Statistics, *Use of Nursing Homes,* 1987: 9.
86. Based on the 1985 National Nursing Home Survey. National Center for Health Statistics, *Use of Nursing Homes,* 1987: 9.
87. Pillemer, 1989: 316.
88. Pillemer, 1989: 315.
89. Pillemer, 1989: 317.
90. Pillemer, 1989: 315.
91. Pillemer, 1989: 315.
92. Pillemer, 1989: 317.
93. Pillemer, 1989: 315.
94. Pillemer, 1989: 316.
95. Pillemer, 1989: 315.
96. Pillemer, 1989: 317.
97. Pillemer, 1989: 315.
98. Pillemer, 1989: 315.
99. Pillemer, 1989: 315.
100. Pillemer, 1989: 315.
101. Data are for 1988 and were prepared by the Older Women's League (OWL) and the American Federation of State, County, and Municipal Employees. Reported in *Older Americans Reports,* October 28, 1988.

102. Data are for 1988 and were prepared by the Older Women's League (OWL) and the American Federation of State, County and Municipal Employees. Reported in *Older Americans Reports,* October 28, 1988.
103. Survey conducted by Louis Harris and Associates. Reported in American Association of Retired Persons (AARP), *Changing Needs,* undated: 122.
104. Survey conducted by Louis Harris and Associates. Reported in American Association of Retired Persons (AARP), *Changing Needs,* undated: 122.
105. Survey conducted by Louis Harris and Associates. Reported in American Association of Retired Persons (AARP), *Changing Needs,* undated: 122.
106. Survey conducted by the Health Insurance Association of America for the University of Maryland Center on Aging. Reported in *Mature Market Report,* April 1989: 1.
107. Survey conducted by the Health Insurance Association of America for the University of Maryland Center on Aging. Reported in *Mature Market Report,* April 1989: 1.
108. Coughlin, 1989: 173.
109. U.S. House of Representatives, Committee on Ways and Means, 1989: 142.
110. *Mature Market Report,* March 1989: 9.
111. *Mature Market Report,* March 1989: 9.
112. Nassif, 1986–87: 6.

Chapter 16

Paying for Health Care

Concern about Health Care Costs

Most Seniors Worry

Percentage of older people who say they worry about medical care costs: 69.[1]

Percentage of Americans of all ages who rate the cost of medical care as the most serious economic and social issue: 52.[2]

Percentage of seniors who agree that "health care costs will take a great portion of my assets": 68.[3]

Health Insurance Coverage

Medicare and Medicaid

The percentage of seniors covered by Medicare: 97.[4]

The number of seniors enrolled in Medicare's Part A: 29.4 million.[5] (Medicare's Part A helps pay for services qualified individuals receive in a hospital, skilled nursing facility, home-health agency, or hospice program.)

The number of seniors who received Part A–reimbursed services under Medicare in 1989: 6.7 million.[6]

The number of seniors enrolled in Medicare's Part B: 29.2 million.[7] (Medicare's Part B helps to pay for covered services provided by a doctor and a wide range of medical services clients use when they are not patients in hospitals.)

The number of seniors who received Part B–reimbursed services under Medicare in 1989: 23.6 million.[8]

The percentage of seniors who receive Medicaid: 12.[9]

The number of seniors in 1987 who received Medicaid vendor payments: 3,260,328.[10]

Percentage of seniors who receive both Medicare and Medicaid: 10.[11]

Percentage of senior Medicare enrollees who are expected to benefit from the new Medicaid "buy-in" requirement (under which Medicare premiums and co-payment costs are picked up by Medicaid for poor persons who do not receive Medicaid): 8.[12]

Institutions and Organizations Participating in Medicare in 1988

The number of hospitals participating in Medicare: 6,715.[13]

The number of skilled nursing facilities: 7,379.[14]

The number of home health care agencies: 5,769.[15]

The number of hospices: 449.[16]

The percentage of physicians who do *not* participate in Medicare's assignment program: 60.[17]

Most Seniors Not Knowledgeable about Medicare

Percentage of seniors who are unaware of or incorrect about their Medicare coverage, according to a telephone survey of 400 seniors in Minnesota: 92.[18]

Percentage who are unaware of or are incorrect about whether Medicare covers in-home medical care: 71.[19]

Percentage who do not know or are incorrect about whether Medicare covers in-home daily routine care: 58.[20]

Percentage who do not know or are incorrect about whether Medicare covers routine physical exams and X rays: 83.[21]

Percentage who do not know if Medicare covers short-term nursing home care: 43.[22]

Paying for Medicare

The monthly premium in 1990 for enrolling in Medicare Part A for those not automatically covered: $175.[23]

The monthly Medicare Part B premium in 1990: $28.60.[24]

The payroll tax in 1990 for the Hospital Insurance Trust Fund, which finances Part A of Medicare: 1.45 percent of earnings up to $51,300 per employee with the employer making an equal contribution.[25]

Majority of Seniors Have Medicare Supplemental Insurance

The percentage of seniors who have Medicare supplemental insurance: 82.[26]

The number of older Americans who cannot afford to buy insurance to supplement Medicare: more than 3 million.[27]

The percentage of retired persons age 55 and over who have employer-provided health benefits: 49.[28]

Many Seniors Confused about Supplemental Health Coverage

Percentage of seniors who are confused about their private supplemental health insurance, according to a telephone survey of 400 seniors in Minnesota: 50.[29]

Percentage who do not know if their supplemental insurance covers in-home medical care: 42.[30]

Percentage who are unsure about whether their supplemental insurance covers in-home supportive care: 39.[31]

Percentage who are unsure about whether it covers short-term nursing home care: 42.[32]

Percentage who do not know if it covers long-term nursing home stays: 46.[33]

Most Seniors Can't Afford Nursing Home Insurance

Percentage of seniors between the ages of 65 and 79 who cannot afford to pay for the *average cost* of basic nursing home insurance policies: 84.[34]

Percentage in this age group who cannot afford to buy the lowest-priced policies: 73.[35]

Health Care Expenditures

Health Care Spending Outpaces Growth of GNP

Growth in aggregate personal health care expenditures from 1977 to 1987: 11.5 percent per year.[36]

Compared to growth in the gross national product: an 8.6 percent growth rate.[37]

Growth in consumption of health care spending by the elderly from 1977 to 1987: 13.6 percent annually.[38]

Billions Spent for Personal Health Care

The total amount spent for personal health care for seniors in 1987: $162 billion.[39]

Medicare outlays in 1988: $81.6 billion.[40]

Out of every dollar spent on personal health care in the United States, the amount spent for or by seniors: 36 cents.[41]

Percentage of Medicare funds that goes to people with less than one year to live: 28.[42]

Per Capita Spending

Per capita spending for personal health care for seniors in 1987: $5,360.[43]

Compared to per capita spending for younger persons: $1,286.[44]

The average amount that seniors spent out of their own pockets or through other private sources in 1987: $2,004.[45]

The amount spent by Medicare per senior: $2,391.[46]

The amount spent by Medicaid per senior: $645.[47]

The amount spent by other sources: $321.[48]

Out of every dollar spent on personal health care by seniors, the amount seniors cover out of their own pockets or through other private sources: 37 cents.[49]

The amount covered by Medicare: 45 cents.[50]

The amount covered by Medicaid: 12 cents.[51]

The amount covered by other sources: 6 cents.[52]

Every Day in the United States

Seniors spend $5.50 per day out of their own pockets or through other private sources for personal health care.[53]

And Medicare spends $6.55 for personal health care for seniors.[54]

Health Care Spending Greatest for Oldest-Old

Per capita personal health care spending for the oldest-old (85-plus) compared to persons age 65 to 69: spending for the oldest-old is two and one-half times greater.[55]

Per capita personal health care spending by the oldest-old for nursing home care compared to spending for persons age 65 to 69: spending for the oldest-old is 23 times greater.[56]

Per capita personal health care spending for the oldest-old: $9,178.[57]

Compared to spending for persons age 65 to 69: $3,728.[58]

The average amount of money that the oldest-old spend for health care per day out of their own pockets or through other private sources: $10.[59]

Medicare's share of per capita spending for the oldest-old: 35 percent.[60]

Compared to persons age 65 to 69: 50 percent.[61]

The percentage of personal health care spending for the oldest-old that is out-of-pocket and from other private sources: 40.[62]

Compared to persons age 65 to 69: 38 percent.[63]

The percentage of personal health care spending for the oldest-old covered by Medicaid: 19.[64]

Compared to persons age 65 to 69: 7.[65]

Overall, Medicaid spending for the oldest-old in relation to spending for persons age 65 to 69 is: seven times greater.[66]

What Is Spent for Physicians, Hospitals, Nursing Homes, and Prescription Drugs

Spending for Physician Services

Annual growth rate of spending for physician services from 1977 to 1987: 12.4 percent.[67]

Amount spent for physician services for seniors in 1987: $33.5 billion.[68]

Per capita spending by seniors for physician care in 1987: $1,107.[69]

Out of every dollar spent on physician services for seniors, the amount seniors cover out of their own pockets or through other private sources: 36 cents.[70]

The amount that Medicare pays: 61 cents.[71]

The amount that Medicaid pays: 2 cents.[72]

Spending for Hospital Services

Annual growth rate of spending for hospital services from 1977 to 1987: 11.1 percent.[73]

Amount spent for hospital care for seniors in 1987: $67.9 billion.[74]

Per capita spending by seniors for hospital care in 1987: $2,248.[75]

Out of every dollar spent on hospital services for seniors, the amount seniors cover out of their own pockets or through other private sources: 15 cents.[76]

The amount that Medicare pays: 70 cents.[77]

The amount that Medicaid pays: 5 cents.[78]

Spending for Nursing Home Care

Annual growth rate of spending for nursing home care from 1977 to 1987: 12.1 percent.[79]

Aggregate nursing home care expenditures in 1987: $40.6 billion.[80]

Per capita spending by seniors for nursing home care in 1987: $1,085.[81]

Out of every dollar spent on nursing home services for seniors, the amount seniors cover out of their own pockets or through other private sources: 58 cents.[82]

The amount that Medicare pays: 2 cents.[83]

The amount that Medicaid pays: 36 cents.[84]

The percentage of personal health care spending for those age 85 and over that goes toward nursing home care: 41.[85]

The percentage for those age 65 to 69: 4.[86]

Spending for Prescription Drugs

The amount of money seniors spent in 1986 for prescription drugs: $9 billion.[87]

The percentage that was paid out-of-pocket: 81.[88]

Notes

1. Study by *Money* magazine. Reported in *Mature Market Report,* May 1989: 9.
2. Survey of 5,000 households by National Family Opinion Inc. for the Conference Board. Conference Board, "The Issues of Public Concern," August 1988.
3. Survey of 1,000 households in the senior and middle generations conducted by New World Decisions for Transamerica Life Companies. Transamerica Life Companies, 1988: 2.
4. U.S. Senate Special Committee on Aging, *Aging America,* 1987: 66.
5. Data are for 1989. U.S. House of Representatives, Committee on Ways and Means, 1989: 127.
6. Data are for 1989. U.S. House of Representatives, Committee on Ways and Means, 1989: 127.
7. Data are for 1989. U.S. House of Representatives, Committee on Ways and Means, 1989: 127.
8. Data are for 1989. U.S. House of Representatives, Committee on Ways and Means, 1989: 127.
9. U.S. Senate Special Committee on Aging, *Aging America,* 1987: 66.
10. U.S. Department of Health and Human Services, *Medicaid Medical Vendor Payments,* 1988.
11. U.S. House of Representatives, Committee on Ways and Means, 1989: 221.
12. U.S. House of Representatives, Committee on Ways and Means, 1989: 221.
13. U.S. House of Representatives, Committee on Ways and Means, 1989: 138.
14. U.S. House of Representatives, Committee on Ways and Means, 1989: 138.
15. U.S. House of Representatives, Committee on Ways and Means, 1989: 138.
16. U.S. House of Representatives, Committee on Ways and Means, 1989: 138.
17. U.S. House of Representatives, Committee on Ways and Means, 1989: 385.
18. Telephone survey by C. J. Olson Research for Seniors Plus. Reported in *Older Americans Reports,* July 10, 1987: 6.
19. Telephone survey by C. J. Olson Research for Seniors Plus. Reported in *Older Americans Reports,* July 10, 1987: 6.
20. Telephone survey by C. J. Olson Research for Seniors Plus. Reported in *Older Americans Reports,* July 10, 1987: 6.
21. Telephone survey by C. J. Olson Research for Seniors Plus. Reported in *Older Americans Reports,* July 10, 1987: 6.
22. Telephone survey by C. J. Olson Research for Seniors Plus. Reported in *Older Americans Reports,* July 10, 1987: 6.
23. Data supplied by the Health Care Financing Administration.
24. Data supplied by the Health Care Financing Administration.

25. U.S. House of Representatives, Committee on Ways and Means, 1989: 147.
26. Survey by the American Association of Retired Persons. Reported in *Older Americans Reports,* January 26, 1990: 35.
27. Survey by American Association of Retired Persons. *Older Americans Reports,* January 26, 1990: 35.
28. Data from the National Center for Health Services Research reported in *Older Americans Reports,* January 5, 1990: 6.
29. Families USA, 1990: 5.
30. Families USA, 1990: 5.
31. Telephone survey by C. J. Olson Research for Seniors Plus. Reported in *Older Americans Reports,* July 10, 1987: 6.
32. Telephone survey by C. J. Olson Research for Seniors Plus. Reported in *Older Americans Reports,* July 10, 1987: 6.
33. Telephone survey by C. J. Olson Research for Seniors Plus. Reported in *Older Americans Reports,* July 10, 1987: 6.
34. Telephone survey by C. J. Olson Research for Seniors Plus. Reported in *Older Americans Reports,* July 10, 1987: 6.
35. Telephone survey by C. J. Olson Research for Seniors Plus. Reported in *Older Americans Reports,* July 10, 1987: 6.
36. Personal health care expenditures are defined as spending for the direct consumption of health care goods and services. Waldo, 1989: 111.
37. Waldo, 1989: 111.
38. Waldo, 1989: 112.
39. Waldo, 1989: 111.
40. U.S. House of Representatives, Committee on Ways and Means, 1989: 152.
41. Waldo, 1989: 111.
42. Health Care Financing Administration. Reported in Lapham, 1987: 56.
43. Waldo, 1989: 111.
44. Waldo, 1989: 114.
45. Waldo, 1989: 118.
46. Waldo, 1989: 118.
47. Waldo, 1989: 118.
48. Waldo, 1989: 118.
49. Waldo, 1989: 118.
50. Waldo, 1989: 118.
51. Waldo, 1989: 118.
52. Waldo, 1989: 118.
53. Based on Waldo, 1989: 118.
54. Based on Waldo, 1989: 118.
55. Waldo, 1989: 114.
56. Waldo, 1989: 114.
57. Waldo, 1989: 118.
58. Waldo, 1989: 118.
59. Based on Waldo, 1989: 118.
60. Waldo, 1989: 118.
61. Waldo, 1989: 118.
62. Waldo, 1989: 118.
63. Waldo, 1989: 118.
64. Waldo, 1989: 118.

65. Waldo, 1989: 118.
66. Waldo, 1989: 114.
67. Waldo, 1989: 112.
68. Waldo, 1989: 112.
69. Waldo, 1989: 118.
70. Waldo, 1989: 118.
71. Waldo, 1989: 118.
72. Waldo, 1989: 118.
73. Waldo, 1989: 112.
74. Waldo, 1989: 112.
75. Waldo, 1989: 118.
76. Waldo, 1989: 118.
77. Waldo, 1989: 118.
78. Waldo, 1989: 118.
79. Waldo, 1989: 112.
80. Waldo, 1989: 112.
81. Waldo, 1989: 118.
82. Waldo, 1989: 114.
83. Waldo, 1989: 114.
84. Waldo, 1989: 114.
85. Waldo, 1989: 114.
86. Waldo, 1989: 114.
87. *Mature Market Report,* August/September 1989: 7.
88. *Mature Market Report,* August/September 1989: 7.

Chapter 17

Attitudes of and toward Seniors

Feelings toward Government and the Power Structure

Many Feel Alienated

Percentage of older Americans who report that they currently feel alienated from the power structure: 64.[1]

Compared to 1966: 32 percent felt alienated.[2]

Most Seniors Feel Government Should Care for Needy

Percentage of seniors who agree with the statement: "The government has a basic responsibility to take care of people who can't take care of themselves": 81.[3]

Percentage who disagree: 12.[4]

Percentage who are not sure: 7.[5]

Percentage who agree with the statement: "Government should guarantee that every citizen has enough to eat and a place to live": 67.[6]

Percentage who disagree: 24.[7]

Percentage who are not sure: 9.[8]

Percentage who agree with the statement: "The government is spending too much money on programs to help the poor": 23.[9]

Percentage who disagree: 63.[10]

Percentage who are not sure: 14.[11]

Percentage who agree with the statement: "The government and individual Americans have special responsibilities to spend money helping the poor in other countries": 34.[12]

Percentage who disagree: 56.[13]

Percentage who are not sure: 10.[14]

Most Americans Favor Spending for Seniors

According to a Conference Board Survey, the portion of Americans who oppose cutbacks in government spending for Social Security, Medicare, and veterans' benefits: 4 in 5.[15]

Compared to those who want a cut in foreign aid: more than 9 in 10.[16]

Percentage of Americans who oppose cutbacks in spending for Social Security: 86.[17]

Percentage who oppose cutting Medicare: 82.[18]

Percentage who oppose cutting veterans' benefits: 79.[19]

Most Americans Feel Government Should Help Provide More Housing for Seniors

Americans who agree that more housing is needed for low- and moderate-income elderly: 89 percent.[20]

Percentage who agree that the federal government should help finance the development of such housing: 73.[21]

Most Americans Feel Government Should Provide Long-Term Care

Americans who feel that long-term care is an extremely important issue in our country today: nearly half.[22]

Americans who favor a federal government program to provide long-term care to chronically ill and disabled seniors, adults, and children: more than 8 in 10.[23]

Americans who say they would support a specific tax on the wealthy—eliminating the limit on the amount of earnings subject to the 1.45 percent Medicare payroll tax—to pay for the program: more than 7 in 10.[24]

Percentage of Americans who believe that they cannot afford the cost of long-term care at home or in a nursing home: 82.[25]

Percentage of people over age 45 who support an increase in federal spending for long-term care for the elderly and disabled: 73.[26]

Percentage who want spending held at current levels: 21.[27]

Portion who support the creation of a new federal program that would pay for long-term care for the elderly and disabled: more than 4 in 5.[28]

Americans who want the government to help pay for long-term care, rather than leave it entirely to the family: 86 percent.[29]

Percentage who say they would be willing to pay for a long-term care program with increased taxes: 68.[30]

Senior Attitudes about Life

Most Seniors Satisfied

According to a poll by Lou Harris and Associates, the percentage of persons 50 to 64 who say that they feel satisfied with life: 73.[31]

Percentage of those 65 and over: 72.[32]

Another Harris poll found that at any given moment:

- 82 percent of seniors do *not* experience frequent difficulties.[33]

- 69 percent do *not* face a serious problem in their life and[34]

- 60 percent do not have some fear about the future that worries them a lot.[35]

And according to another poll by the *Los Angeles Times,* Americans over 65 are far happier with their lives than younger people. Seniors who said that they are "quite pleased with the way things are going" in their personal lives: nearly two-thirds.[36]

Compared to persons age 18 to 49: about half.[37]

(The poll also found that: the older people are, the less concerned they are about money or retirement, the less likely they are to be lonely or depressed, and the less fearful they are of disease and death.[38])

Lear's Survey of Women's Attitudes

Lou Harris and Associates and *Lear's* magazine interviewed 700 college-educated women nationwide from age 40 to 65, each with a household income of at least $40,000. The following includes the results reported for women age 60 to 65:

The following increase with age: sense of success, of eloquence, of courage, of serenity, of grace, and of attractiveness.[39]

At age 60 to 65 the percentage of women who say they feel younger than men the same age: 59.[40]

Percentage who work for pay: 42.[41]

Percentage reporting that they are energetic: 59.[42]

Percentage reporting a lower energy level: 7.[43]

Percentage reporting that sex is less important than it was: 68.[44]

What Spouses Want from Each Other

In a Veterans Administration study, what senior wives said they want from their husbands: more help with the housework.[45]

What older husbands said they want from their wives: more interesting meals and more frequent sex.[46]

(These results were the same whether the spouse was working or retired.)

Feelings about Finances

Percentage of seniors who agree that the "government will not have adequate resources to meet the needs of its retired citizens in the year 2000": 58.[47]

Percentage of persons over 55 who consider themselves and their families to be better off financially than their parents were at the same age: 57.[48]

Percentage who think they will either attain or surpass the financial success of their parents: 50.[49]

On the other hand, in a survey by the Conference Board the portion of Americans that think that the living standards of seniors have worsened in the last eight years: half.[50]

The percentage of seniors who say that having too many medical bills is a serious problem for them: 17.[51]

The percentage who say that not having enough money to live on in general is a serious problem for them: 14.[52]

The percentage who say they worry a lot about not having enough money to live on at the present time: 17.[53]

Percentage of Americans aged 50 to 64 who think children should be sure their elderly parents have adequate income: 28.[54]

Attitudes about Aging and Death

Older People Worry Less about Dying

Percentage of persons over 65 who worry about death: 24.[55]

Compared to people age 18 to 24: 55 percent.[56]

Most Seniors Comfortable with Their Age

Percentage of seniors who say they like the age they are: 61.[57]

Percentage of men who would like to find a way not to show the evidence of aging: 27.[58]

Percentage of women who would like to make changes to cover up telltale signs of aging: 48.[59]

Percentage of Americans who think they look younger than they are: 57.[60]

Percentage of Americans who say they feel young for their age: 66.[61]

Percentage of people over 50 who think their greatest achievements are still ahead of them: 23.[62]

Percentage of people over 50 who do not often wish they were teenagers again: 89.[63]

Percentage of Americans who say they want to live to be 100: 49.[64]

Attitudes toward Personal Appearance, Fitness, and Health

Seniors Value Health

Percentage of seniors who say they would trade two years of life for one year of good health: 86.[65]

In defining health, seniors rated the following in order of importance:

- Freedom from pain
- Ability to walk
- Mental alertness
- Good vision
- Good hearing
- Independence[66]

Percentage who give a high priority to diet and nutrition: 58.[67]

Percentage who give a high priority to health and fitness: 52.[68]

Percentage of seniors who say they worry a lot about being in poor health: 18.[69]

Percentage of seniors who say they sometimes stay in bed most of the day: 12.[70]

Percentage of seniors who if told that they were likely to get an incurable illness due to defective genes would refuse to undergo genetic engineering: 45.[71]

Percentage of Americans who would not take a test that indicated whether they were likely to develop a fatal disease in later life: 29.[72]

Looking and Feeling Good

Percentage of persons over 50 who express support for focusing on self-enhancement: 52.[73]

Percentage who say that they have a strong need to do things to look and feel good: 62.[74]

The percentage who find ways to relieve pressure and stress: 46.[75]

Percentage using skin care products: 25.[76]

Percentage using products that "make me look and feel good": 37.[77]

Percentage who say they have a strong need to keep up with trends in fashion: 20.[78]

Notes

1. Harris, 1987: 37.
2. Harris, 1987: 37.
3. Independent Sector, 1988: 57.
4. Independent Sector, 1988: 57.
5. Independent Sector, 1988: 57.
6. Independent Sector, 1988: 58.
7. Independent Sector, 1988: 58.
8. Independent Sector, 1988: 58.
9. Independent Sector, 1988: 59.
10. Independent Sector, 1988: 59.
11. Independent Sector, 1988: 59.
12. Independent Sector, 1988: 60.
13. Independent Sector, 1988: 60.
14. Independent Sector, 1988: 60.
15. Survey of 5,000 households by National Family Opinion Inc. for the Conference Board. Conference Board, "The Public View," 1988 (unpaginated).
16. Conference Board, "The Public View," 1988 (unpaginated).
17. The Conference Board, "The Public View," 1988 (unpaginated).
18. The Conference Board, "The Public View," 1988 (unpaginated).
19. The Conference Board, "The Public View," 1988 (unpaginated).
20. Survey of 1,015 people by the American Association of Retired Persons. Reported in *Older Americans Reports,* March 30, 1990: 126.
21. Survey of 1,015 people by the American Association of Retired Persons. Reported in *Older Americans Reports*, March 30, 1990: 126.
22. Survey conducted by the Health Insurance Association of America for the University of Maryland Center on Aging. Reported in *Mature Market Report,* April 1989: 1.
23. Survey of 1,500 adult Americans by Lou Harris and Associates. Reported in *Older Americans Reports,* April 1, 1988: 131. A similar survey conducted for the Long-Term Care Campaign found that six out of seven respondents believe it is time to consider some government program for long-term care.
24. Survey of 1,500 adult Americans by Lou Harris and Associates. Reported in *Older Americans Reports,* April 1, 1988: 131.
25. Survey by Louis Harris and Associates. Reported in American Association of Retired Persons (AARP), *Changing Needs,* undated: 123.
26. Survey by Hamilton, Frederick, and Schneider. Reported in the American Association of Retired Persons (AARP), *Changing Needs,* undated: 119.

27. Survey by Hamilton, Frederick, and Schneider. Reported in the American Association of Retired Persons (AARP), *Changing Needs,* undated: 119.

28. Survey by Hamilton, Frederick, and Schneider. Reported in the American Association of Retired Persons (AARP), *Changing Needs:* 119.

29. Survey by R. L. Associates for the American Association of Retired Persons and the Villers Foundation. Reported in the American Association of Retired Persons (AARP), *Changing Needs,* undated: 120.

30. Survey by R. L. Associates for the American Association of Retired Persons and the Villers Foundation. Reported in the American Association of Retired Persons (AARP), *Changing Needs,* undated: 120.

31. Harris, 1987: 39.

32. Harris, 1987: 39.

33. Harris, 1986: 45.

34. Harris, 1986: 45.

35. Harris, 1986: 45.

36. Poll by the *Los Angeles Times.* Reported in *Older Americans Reports,* May 12, 1989: 189.

37. Poll by the *Los Angeles Times.* Reported in *Older Americans Reports,* May 12, 1989: 189.

38. Poll by the *Los Angeles Times.* Reported in *Older Americans Reports,* May 12, 1989: 189.

39. Bowe, 1989: 68.

40. Bowe, 1989: 66.

41. Bowe, 1989: 66.

42. Bowe, 1989: 68.

43. Bowe, 1989: 68.

44. Bowe, 1989: 64.

45. Study by David Eckerdt and Barbara Vinick. Reported in *Mature Market Report,* February 1989.

46. Study by David Eckerdt and Barbara Vinick. Reported in *Mature Market Report,* February 1989.

47. Survey of 1,000 adults conducted by New World Decisions for Transamerica Life Companies. Transamerica Life Companies, 1988: 3.

48. *Mature Outlook,* 1988: 79.

49. *Mature Outlook,* 1988: 79.

50. *Older Americans Reports,* November 18, 1988: 459.

51. Harris, 1986: 43.

52. Harris, 1986: 43.

53. Harris, 1986: 43.

54. Weiss, *100%,* 1988 (unpaginated).

55. A *USA Today* poll. Reported in *Mature Market Report,* July 1988: 7.

56. A *USA Today* poll. Reported in *Mature Market Report,* July 1988: 7.

57. A *USA Today* poll. Reported in *Mature Market Report,* July 1988: 7.

58. Harris, 1987: 5.

59. Harris, 1987: 5.

60. John Deere and Co. Reported in Lapham, 1987: 6.

61. ABC News and *Washington Post* poll. Reported in Lapham, 1987: 27.

62. R. H. Bruskin Associates. Reported in Weiss, *100%,* 1988 (unpaginated).

63. R. H. Bruskin Associates. Reported in Weiss, *100%,* 1988 (unpaginated).

64. Media General and Associated Press poll. Reported in Lapham, 1987: 4.
65. Survey conducted by Clayton Davis and Assoc. for the American Chiropractic Association. Reported in *Mature Market Report*, August/September 1989: 9.
66. Survey conducted by Clayton Davis and Assoc. for the American Chiropractic Association. Reported in *Mature Market Report*, August/September 1989: 9.
67. Daniel Yankelovich Group, 1987: 10.
68. Daniel Yankelovich Group, 1987: 10.
69. Harris, 1986: 44.
70. Harris, 1986: 44.
71. Harris, 1987: 138.
72. *Business Week* and Louis Harris and Associates poll. Reported in Weiss, *100%*, 1988 (unpaginated).
73. Daniel Yankelovich Group, 1987: 10.
74. Daniel Yankelovich Group, 1987: 10.
75. Daniel Yankelovich Group, 1987: 10.
76. Daniel Yankelovich Group, 1987: 11.
77. Daniel Yankelovich Group, 1987: 11.
78. Daniel Yankelovich Group, 1987: 14.

Chapter 18

The Growing Senior Market

Going after Senior Dollars

Seniors Account for Billions in Discretionary Income

Share of all consumer dollars that goes to the market over 50: 2 in 5.[1]

Share of discretionary spending dollars: half.[2] (Discretionary income is that income beyond what is needed to maintain a reasonably comfortable standard of living.)

Estimated amount of discretionary income for the 50-plus market in 1985: $130 billion.[3]

Estimated amount for seniors: $46.7 billion.[4]

(Discretionary income is money available for luxuries, goods, and services.)

Appealing to Senior Consumers

According to a poll by the Gallup Organization for *Advertising Age Magazine*, the percentage of consumers over the age of 18 who react positively to advertising that features older people: 77.[5]

Percentage who believe that advertisers are too obsessed with youth: 63.[6]

Percentage who think that advertisers don't use mature adults often enough: 53.[7]

Percentage of people over age 65 who feel that they are misrepresented in ads: 43.[8]

Percentage who think that advertisers are not overly obsessed with youth: 40.[9]

According to an ongoing study of older consumers at Georgia State, the product information that active and healthy older adults most often act upon: information they get from relatives and friends.[10]

According to a study by Donnelly Marketing in Stamford, Connecticut, the advertising media that count with persons age 50 and over ranked in order of preference on a scale of 1 to 5:

- New product trial: 3.6
- Word of mouth: 3.6
- New brand trial: 3.5
- Television/radio: 2.3
- Magazines: 2.3
- Direct mail: 2.3[11]

The preferred terms for describing the 50-plus market:

- Mature: 28 percent
- Adult: 25 percent
- Senior: 24 percent
- 50-plus: 17 percent
- Other: 6 percent[12]

The changes in marketing and design that seniors would like to see:

- Elimination of condescending advertisements
- Packages that open more easily
- Smaller portions and travel sizes
- More emphasis on quality of products and services[13]

50-Plus Consumers and the Media

Persons over 50 Make Up Large Share of Media Users

Percentage of all viewers of prime time television who are 50-plus: 47.[14]

Percentage of early and late fringe television: 51.[15]

Percentage of daytime television: 46.[16]

Percentage of newspaper readers: 37.[17]

Percentage of magazine consumers: 34.[18]

Percentage of readers of *Reader's Digest:* 49.[19]

Percentage of readers of *McCall's* magazine: 44.[20]

Percentage of readers of *Woman's Day:* 41.[21]

Percentage of radio listeners: 32.[22]

Percentage of readers of outdoor billboards: 37.[23]

Percentage of 50-plus persons who go to the movies at least twice a month: nearly 80.[24]

Seniors Are Newspaper Readers

In contrast to the study above, the Newspaper Advertising Bureau found that: 43 percent of newspaper readers are over age 50.[25]

Percentage of these older readers who are among a given newspaper's most loyal and thorough readers: 90.[26]

Percentage who are interested in news about health and medicine: 79.[27]

Percentage interested in finance: 54.[28]

Percentage interested in Social Security: 43.[29]

Percentage interested in recreation and leisure: 26.[30]

Percentage of newspapers that carry a regular column on aging: 47.[31]

Percentage that supply special-interest information for older readers in the general news of the feature sections: 59.[32]

Senior Shoppers

Senior Shopping Habits and Attitudes

The number of hours people 65 and over shop per week: 5.7.[33]

Compared to people age 55 to 64: 6.5 hours.[34]

In a survey of 500 50-plus shoppers by Time Market Research, the percentage who said that poor customer service is the leading barrier to shopping: 46.[35]

Percentage who said that high prices are a deterrent to shopping: 4.[36]

Percentage who preferred a few good items over more items of less quality: 89.[37]

Percentage who would pay more for the same merchandise closer to home: 71.[38]

Where Persons over 50 Shop

Percentage of persons 50 and over who shopped by mail in the last year: 76.[39]

The average amount spent by those who shopped by mail: $290.[40]

Where persons 50 and over shop for linens: 32 percent in chain stores, 15 percent in discount stores.[41]

Where they purchase gifts: 30 percent in department stores, 30 percent in giftware speciality stores.[42]

Where they purchase major appliances in speciality stores: 27 percent in national chains, 8 percent in department stores.[43]

And in a study by Daniel Yankelovich for *Modern Maturity* magazine, the percentage of persons over 50 who express commitment to:

- Brand loyalty: 73
- Quality over cost: 72
- Shopping at stores with the best prices: 76
- Paying a little extra to save time and effort: 61
- Going out of the way to shop at stores that give good service: 54
- Patronizing socially responsible companies: 53
- Shopping at stores that cater to me: 48
- Ordering from catalogs: 16
- Ordering from TV shopping clubs: 5

The percentage who say they will pay more attention to:

- Reading ingredient labels: 56
- Trying new products: 26
- Using carry-out foods: 22 [44]

Taking Advantage of Discounts

Percentage of persons between the ages of 55 and 79 who always take advantage of senior discounts: 13.[45]

Percentage who frequently take advantage of senior discounts: 41.[46]

Percentage who occasionally take advantage of senior discounts: 43.[47]

Percentage who never use age-related discounts: 10.[48]

Seniors Outspend Other Americans on Food

Segment of the population that spends the most per capita on food: people over 65.[49]

Percentage of food expenditures persons between age 55 and 74 spend on eating out: 28.[50]

Percentage people over 75 spend: 23.[51]

Number of times per week that seniors eat out: 2.[52]

Percentage of dinners eaten out by persons over age 50 that are in moderately priced restaurants: 40.[53]

The annual senior market for packaged foods: $13 billion.[54]

Projections for the annual senior market for packaged foods in five years: $17.9 billion.[55]

Amount householders over 55 spend on meat purchases, including beef, pork, and poultry: $10.23 per week.[56]

This figure is below average by: 27 percent.[57]

According to a study by the Food Marketing Institute, the percentage of shoppers over age 50 who peruse newspapers for grocery specials before they shop: about half.[58]

Percentage who use price-off coupons: 40.[59]

The average number of times a week 50-plus shoppers visit supermarkets: 1.6.[60]

Percentage of shoppers over 65 who go to supermarkets other than their principal one for advertised specials: 11.[61]

The most important variable in overall shopper satisfaction: service.[62]

Products and Services of Interest to Seniors

According to a study by Donnelly Marketing in Stamford, Connecticut, the products and services that interest persons age 50 and over ranked in order of preference on a scale of 1 to 5:

- Health care: 4.1
- Financial services: 3.7
- Travel: 3.6
- Hobbies: 3.3
- Education: 3.1
- Automobiles: 3.1[63]

Seniors and Services

Majority Would Not Pay for Specified Goods and Services

The *Wall Street Journal*'s "American Way of Buying" survey asked retired respondents what they would be willing to pay for a specific list of goods and services. The result was that a majority was *unwilling* to pay anything at all for any item on the list. Here is the breakdown for specific services:

Percentage of retirees or their spouses who said they would not pay for an annual railway or airline pass for unlimited travel at peak times at a bargain price: 51.[64]

Who would pay a moderate amount or only a little: 43.[65]

Percentage who would not pay for a club membership offering trips for cultural, educational, and recreational purposes: 53.[66]

Who would pay a moderate amount or only a little: 42.[67]

Percentage who would not pay for a car and driver to take them shopping, to restaurants, and to see friends: 64.[68]

Who would pay a moderate amount or only a little: 30.[69]

Percentage who would not pay for a service to do the laundry and clean the house: 51.[70]

Who would pay a moderate amount or only a little: 42.[71]

Percentage who would not pay for a service to do food shopping for them: 68.[72]

Who would pay a moderate amount or only a little: 27.[73]

Percentage who would not pay for someone to come or phone every day to make sure they are all right: 64.[74]

Who would pay a moderate amount or only a little: 28.[75]

Percentage who would not pay for someone to deliver hot meals to them every day: 57.[76]

Who would pay a moderate amount or only a little: 35.[77]

Percentage who would not pay for a financial adviser who understands the circumstances of a retired person: 73.[78]

Who would pay a moderate amount or only a little: 21.[79]

Percentage who would not pay for a place to buy special foods low in salt, cholesterol, sugar, fat, or calories: 60.[80]

Who would pay a moderate amount or only a little: 32.[81]

Percentage who would not pay for a fitness and exercise class: 73.[82]

Who would pay a moderate amount or only a little: 22.[83]

Notes

1. Consumer Research Center, 1985: 3.
2. Consumer Research Center, 1985: 3.
3. Consumer Research Center, 1985: 8.
4. Consumer Research Center, 1985: 8.
5. Ward, 1989: S-1.
6. Ward, 1989: S-1.
7. Ward, 1989: S-1.
8. Ward, 1989: S-2.
9. Ward, 1989: S-2.
10. *Mature Market Report,* April 1989: 5.
11. Study by Richard Balkite of Donnelly Marketing. Reported in *Mature Market Report,* May 1988.
12. Study by Richard Balkite of Donnelly Marketing. Reported in *Mature Market Report,* May 1988.
13. Study by Richard Balkite of Donnelly Marketing. Reported in *Mature Market Report,* May 1988.
14. Simmons Market Research Bureau. Reported in *Mature Market Report,* April 1988: 3.

15. Simmons Market Research Bureau. Reported in *Mature Market Report*, April 1988: 3.
16. Simmons Market Research Bureau. Reported in *Mature Market Report*, April 1988: 3.
17. Simmons Market Research Bureau. Reported in *Mature Market Report*, April 1988: 3.
18. Simmons Market Research Bureau. Reported in *Mature Market Report*, April 1988: 3.
19. Simmons Market Research Bureau. Reported in *Mature Market Report*, April 1988: 3.
20. Simmons Market Research Bureau. Reported in *Mature Market Report*, April 1988: 3.
21. Simmons Market Research Bureau. Reported in *Mature Market Report*, April 1988: 3.
22. Simmons Market Research Bureau. Reported in *Mature Market Report*, April 1988: 3.
23. Simmons Market Research Bureau. Reported in *Mature Market Report*, April 1988: 3.
24. Survey by California Senior Life. Reported in *Mature Market Report*, July 1988: 4.
25. Study by the Newspaper Advertising Bureau. Reported in *Mature Market Report*, March 1988: 9.
26. Study by the Newspaper Advertising Bureau. Reported in *Mature Market Report*, March 1988: 9.
27. Study by the Newspaper Advertising Bureau. Reported in *Mature Market Report*, March 1988: 9.
28. Study by the Newspaper Advertising Bureau. Reported in *Mature Market Report*, March 1988: 9.
29. Study by the Newspaper Advertising Bureau. Reported in *Mature Market Report*, March 1988: 9.
30. Study by the Newspaper Advertising Bureau. Reported in *Mature Market Report*, March 1988: 9.
31. Study by the Newspaper Advertising Bureau. Reported in *Mature Market Report*, March 1988: 9.
32. Study by the Newspaper Advertising Bureau. Reported in *Mature Market Report*, March 1988: 9.
33. *Mature Market Report*, February 1989: 9.
34. *Mature Market Report*, February 1989: 9.
35. Survey by Time Market Research for Meretrends. Reported in *Mature Market Report*, June 1988: 9.
36. Survey by Time Market Research for Meretrends. Reported in *Mature Market Report*, June 1988: 9.
37. Survey by Time Market Research for Meretrends. Reported in *Mature Market Report*, June 1988: 9.
38. Survey by Time Market Research for Meretrends. Reported in *Mature Market Report*, June 1988: 9.
39. Survey by Time Market Research for Meretrends. Reported in *Mature Market Report*, June 1988: 9.
40. Survey by Time Market Research for Meretrends. Reported in *Mature Market Report*, June 1988: 9.

41. Survey by Time Market Research for Meretrends. Reported in *Mature Market Report,* June 1988: 9.
42. Survey by Time Market Research for Meretrends. Reported in *Mature Market Report,* June 1988: 9.
43. Survey by Time Market Research for Meretrends. Reported in *Mature Market Report,* June 1988: 9.
44. Daniel Yankelovich Group, 1987: 19.
45. Survey by AgeAware. Reported in *Mature Market Report,* May 1989: 3.
46. Survey by AgeAware. Reported in *Mature Market Report,* May 1989: 3.
47. Survey by AgeAware. Reported in *Mature Market Report,* May 1989: 3.
48. Survey by AgeAware. Reported in *Mature Market Report,* May 1989: 3.
49. Study by Frost and Sullivan. Reported in *Mature Market Report,* February 1989: 12.
50. Bureau of Labor Statistics, *Consumer Expenditure Survey.* Reported in *Mature Market Report,* December, 1987: 7.
51. Bureau of Labor Statistics, *Consumer Expenditure Survey.* Reported in *Mature Market Report,* December, 1987: 7.
52. Study by the National Restaurant Association. Reported in *Mature Market Report,* February 1988: 9.
53. Study by Frost and Sullivan. Reported in *Mature Market Report,* February 1989: 12.
54. Study by Frost and Sullivan. Reported in *Mature Market Report,* February 1989: 12.
55. *Mature Market Report,* July 1988: 7.
56. *Mature Market Report,* July 1988: 7.
57. *Mature Market Report,* February 1988: 9.
58. Study by the Food Marketing Institute. Reported in *Mature Market Report,* July 1988: 4.
59. Study by the Food Marketing Institute. Reported in *Mature Market Report,* July 1988: 4.
60. Study by the Food Marketing Institute. Reported in *Mature Market Report,* July 1988: 4.
61. Study by the Food Marketing Institute. Reported in *Mature Market Report,* July 1988: 4.
62. Study by the Food Marketing Institute. Reported in *Mature Market Report,* July 1988: 4.
63. Study by Richard Balkite of Donnelly Marketing. Reported in *Mature Market Report,* May 1988.
64. Carlson, 1989: B1.
65. Carlson, 1989: B1.
66. Carlson, 1989: B1.
67. Carlson, 1989: B1.
68. Carlson, 1989: B1.
69. Carlson, 1989: B1.
70. Carlson, 1989: B1.
71. Carlson, 1989: B1.
72. Carlson, 1989: B1.
73. Carlson, 1989: B1.
74. Carlson, 1989: B1.

75. Carlson, 1989: B1.
76. Carlson, 1989: B1.
77. Carlson, 1989: B1.
78. Carlson, 1989: B1.
79. Carlson, 1989: B1.
80. Carlson, 1989: B1.
81. Carlson, 1989: B1.
82. Carlson, 1989: B1.
83. Carlson, 1989: B1.

Chapter 19

Federal Government Spending for Seniors

Seniors Have Large Share of Federal Budget

Almost One in Three Federal Dollars Goes to Seniors

The percent of the federal budget spent on seniors in 1960: less than 15.[1]

The percent spent in fiscal year 1989: 29 (up from 28 percent in fiscal year 1984).[2]

Federal spending that benefited seniors in fiscal year 1989: $326 billion.[3]

Of every dollar spent on seniors through the federal budget: 84 cents goes to Social Security, Medicare, and Medicaid.[4]

In 1990, the government program that will outdo defense spending for the first time: Social Security.[5]

At current growth rates the government program that will be the largest component of the federal budget in the year 2000: Medicare.[6]

Spending Trends

Portion of federal outlays for seniors spent on retirement income today as compared to 1960: 66 versus 90 percent.[7]

Portion of federal outlays for seniors spent on health programs today as compared to 1960: 29 versus 6 percent.[8]

How the Money Is Spent

Portion of every federal dollar spent on seniors that goes toward Social Security: 56 cents.[9]

Portion that goes toward Medicare: 24 cents.[10]

Portion that goes toward Medicaid: 4 cents.[11]

Portion that goes toward other health costs: 2 cents.[12]

Portion that goes toward housing: 2 cents.[13]

Portion that goes toward benefits for retired federal and military workers: 9 cents.[14]

Portion that goes toward Supplemental Security Income (SSI): 1 cent.[15]

Portion that goes toward programs of general benefit to the elderly such as food stamps, legal services, energy assistance, weatherization, social services, nutrition, and employment services provided through the Older Americans Act, research conducted through the National Institute on Aging, and volunteer services through the ACTION agency: 2 cents.[16]

Social Security and Medicare: Solvency

According to the Social Security Trustees: the income of the Social Security Trust Funds will exceed outlays through the second decade of the next century.[17]

According to Social Security Commissioner Gwendolyn King, the Social Security Administration is taking in $89,000 more each minute than it is taking out.[18]

The U.S. House of Representatives Committee on Ways and Means projects that the Hospital Insurance Trust Fund (Part A of Medicare) will be insolvent in: 2006.[19]

Notes

1. U.S. Senate Special Committee on Aging, *Aging America*, 1988: 154.

2. Chambers Associates, 1989: 2.

3. Chambers Associates, 1989: 2.
4. Chambers Associates, 1989: 4–5.
5. Weinberg, 1989: 18.
6. Seib, 1989: A16
7. Chambers Associates, 1989: 4–5.
8. Chambers Associates, 1989: 4–5.
9. Chambers Associates, 1989: 4–5.
10. Chambers Associates, 1989: 4–5.
11. Chambers Associates, 1989: 4–5.
12. Chambers Associates, 1989: 4–5.
13. Chambers Associates, 1989: 4–5.
14. Chambers Associates, 1989: 4–5.
15. Chambers Associates, 1989: 4–5.
16. Chambers Associates, 1989: 4–5.
17. The U.S. House of Representatives, Committee on Ways and Means, 1989: 81.
18. *USA Today,* October 9, 1989: 31 A.
19. The U.S. House of Representatives, Committee on Ways and Means, 1989: 155.

Chapter 20

World Records and Other Fascinating Facts

The Longest Lives

The Oldest Living Thing

The oldest living thing: "King Clone," a creosote plant, estimated to be 11,700 years old.[1]

Record Holders

The longest-living tortoise on record: 152-plus years.[2]

The longest-living nonbacterial creature on record: a quahog, a thick-shelled clam, that had lived 220 years when found in 1982.[3]

The longest-living nonhuman primate: a male orangutan named "Guas" who lived 59 years.[4]

The age at death of the longest-living cow on record: 78 years.[5]

The longest-living marine mammal: Baird's beaked whale with a maximum life span of 70 years.[6]

Longest-living bat: 31 years, 5 months.[7]

Longest-living monkey: 53 years, 8 months.[8]

Longest-living rodent: 27 years, 3 months.[9]

Longest-living antelope: 25 years, 4 months.[10]

Longest-living deer: 26 years, 8 months.[11]

Longest-living marsupial: 26 years.[12]

Longest-living horse: 62 years.[13]

Longest-living thoroughbred racehorse: 42 years.[14]

Longest-living pony: 54 years.[15]

Longest-living insectivore (moles, shrews, and hedgehogs): 16-plus years for a lesser hedgehog-tenrec.[16]

Longest-living dog: 29 years, 5 months.[17]

Longest-living cat: 36 years.[18]

Longest-living bird: 80-plus years.[19]

Longest-living domestic bird: 49 years, 8 months.[20]

Longest-living lizard: 54-plus years.[21]

Longest-living turtle: 152-plus years.[22]

Longest-living amphibian: 55 years.[23]

Longest-living fish: 82 years.[24]

Longest-living goldfish: 40-plus years.[25]

Longest-living spider: 28 years.[26]

Longest-living crustacean: the lobster, at 50 years for very large specimens.[27]

Longest-living insect: splendor beetles, which may remain in the larvae stage for more than 30 years.[28]

Longest-living tree: a bristlecone pine that was found to be 5,100 years old.[29]

Who Lives Longest

The longest-living mammal: homo sapiens.[30]

The second longest-living mammal: the Asiatic elephant.[31]

Average Lifespans

From 1 Day to 100-plus Years

Of an alligator: 55 years.[32]

Of a cat: 15 years.[33]

Of a dog: 8 to 15 years.[34]

Of a dolphin: 65 years.[35]

Of an elephant: 60 years.[36]

Of a facelift: 6 to 10 years.[37]

Of a hippopotamus: 40 years.[38]

Of a human: 75 years.[39]

Of a horse: 30 years.[40]

Of a housefly: 6 weeks.[41]

Of a lion: 25 years.[42]

Of a lobster: up to 50 years.[43]

Of a macaw: 63 years.[44]

Of a mayfly: 1 day.[45]

Of a mouse: 2 to 3 years.[46]

Of an ostrich: 50 years.[47]

Of an owl: 24 years.[48]

Of a pelican: 45 years.[49]

Of a rattlesnake: 18 years.[50]

Of a rabbit: 12 years.[51]

Of a raven: 69 years.[52]

Of a rhinoceros: 70 years.[53]

Of a sheep: 10 to 15 years.[54]

Of a squirrel: 11 years.[55]

Of a trout: 5 to 10 years.[56]

Of a turtle: 100-plus years.[57]

Seniors around the World

290 Million Seniors

The world's senior population in 1987: 290 million.[58]

Rate of growth of the world's senior population: 2.4 percent a year.[59]

The country with the largest number of seniors: China with 53 million.[60]

The country with the highest proportion of seniors: Sweden with 17 percent.[61]

The country with the highest proportion of oldest-old: Sweden with 3.5 percent over 80.[62]

The portion of seniors living in developing countries: over half (54 percent).[63]

The country where residents live the longest: Japan with a life expectancy of 77 years.[64]

Age Is No Barrier

Seniors in High Places

The average age of U.S. Supreme Court justices: 70.[65]

The proportion of state governors over age 55: more than one-third.

The proportion of U.S. representatives over age 60: almost one-fourth.

The proportion of U.S. senators over age 60: almost one-third.

The average age of today's top Fortune 500 executives: 60.

Some Senior Achievers

In 1988, 100-year-old George Abbot opened a play on Broadway.[66]

At 100, Grandma Moses illustrated 'Twas the Night before Christmas.

At 93, George Bernard Shaw wrote the play Far-Fetched Fables.

At 92, George Burns was performing on stage with 86-year-old Bob Hope.

At 90, Pablo Picasso was producing drawings and engravings.

At 90, Bertrand Russell intervened with heads of state during the Cuban missile crisis.

At 90, Duncan McLean won the 1975 World Veterans Olympics silver medal for the 200-meter run.

At 89, Arthur Rubenstein gave one of his greatest recitals at Carnegie Hall.

At 87, Konrad Adenauer was chancellor of West Germany.

At 86, Arturo Toscanini was a vigorous conductor.

At 81, Benjamin Franklin effected the compromise that led to the adoption of the U.S. Constitution.

At 81, Thomas Edison patented his last invention.

In his 80s, Titian was producing some of his finest works.

At 80, Norman Vincent Peale published his 34th book.

At 79, Marc Chagall produced two magnificent murals for the Metropolitan Opera in New York.

At 75, Duke Ellington made his last recording.

At 74, Claude Monet painted his famous Nymphéas water lilies.

At 71, Cecil B. DeMille produced and directed the award-winning *Greatest Show on Earth.*

At 71, Michelangelo was appointed chief architect of St. Peter's Basilica in Rome.

At 70, Verdi finished *Falstaff.*

In his 70s, Frank Lloyd Wright designed many of his masterpieces, including the Solomon R. Guggenheim Museum in New York.

World Records

Oldest couple to divorce: Simon and Ida Stern, 97 and 91.[67]

Oldest bridegroom: Harry Stevens, 103, who married Thelma Lucas, 84 in 1984.[68]

Oldest bride: Winifred Clark, who was married on the day before her 100th birthday to Albert Smith, 80, in South Yorkshire, England.[69]

Longest marriage: 86 years.[70]

Oldest age at which a driver's license has been issued: 104 years.[71]

Oldest age at which a person has been operated on: a hip operation on James H. Brett, Jr. at age 111 in 1960.[72]

Oldest Oscar Winners

Oldest winner, best actor: Henry Fonda, 76, for *On Golden Pond,* 1982.[73]

Oldest winner, best actress: Jessica Tandy, 80, for *Driving Miss Daisy,* 1990.[74]

Oldest Presidents

Inaugurated at age 69: Ronald Reagan.[75]

Inaugurated at age 68: Martin Van Buren.[76]

Inaugurated at age 65: James Buchanan.[77]

Inaugurated at age 64: Zachary Taylor.[78]

Inaugurated at age 62: Dwight David Eisenhower.[79]

Oldest Sports Greats

The oldest person to win an Olympic game: Oscar Swan, who at age 72, won a silver medal for shooting running deer as a member of a Swedish team in 1920.[80]

The oldest Grand Prix winner: Tazio Giorgio Nuvolari of Italy who won at Albi, France, in 1946 at age 53.[81]

The oldest tennis champion to win the USTA Championships or U.S. Open: Margaret du Pont who won the mixed doubles at age 42 in 1960.[82]

The oldest singles champion: Arthur Gore who won at age 41 in 1909.[83]

The oldest golfer to win the U.S. Open: Hale Irwin at age 45 in 1990.

The oldest golfer to win the Masters Tournament in Augusta, Georgia: Jack Nicklaus at age 46 in 1986 when he won for the sixth time.

Oldest baseball player: Leroy "Satchel" Page who pitched three scoreless innings for the Kansas City Athletics at age 59 in 1965.[84]

Oldest pitcher to strike out 300 batters in a season: Nolan Ryan at age 42.[85]

Oldest pitcher to pitch a no-hitter: Nolan Ryan at age 43 in 1990.

Oldest National Football League player: George Blanda at age 48. (He also established a National Football League record for longevity at 26 seasons.)[86]

Oldest National Basketball Association player: Kareem Abdul-Jabbar who ended his career in 1989 at age 42.[87]

Oldest bowling champion: Joe Detloff, who at age 72, won a Booster team event in 1965.[88]

Oldest heavyweight crown holder: Jersey Joe Walcott at age 38. [89]

Oldest female swimmer to conquer the English Channel: Ada Rosina Taylor who crossed the Channel in 1975 at age 45.[90]

Oldest male swimmer to conquer the English Channel: Clifford Batt who crossed the Channel at age 68 in 1987.[91]

In an Average Lifetime . . .

The amount of time spent waiting for traffic lights to change: 5 months.[92]

The amount of time spent on household chores: 4 years.[93]

The amount of time spent eating: 6 years.[94]

The amount of time spent standing in line: 6 years.[95]

Notes

1. *Guinness 1989*, 1988: 69.
2. *Guinness 1989*, 1988: 56.
3. *Guinness 1989*, 1988: 34.
4. *Guinness 1989*, 1988: 40.
5. *Guinness 1989*, 1988: 38.
6. *Guinness 1989*, 1988: 38.
7. *Guinness 1989*, 1988: 40.
8. *Guinness 1989*, 1988: 41.
9. *Guinness 1989*, 1988: 43
10. *Guinness 1989*, 1988: 42.
11. *Guinness 1989*, 1988: 43.
12. *Guinness 1989*, 1988: 44.
13. *Guinness 1989*, 1988: 45.
14. *Guinness 1989*, 1988: 45.
15. *Guinness 1989*, 1988: 45.
16. *Guinness 1989*, 1988: 44.
17. *Guinness 1989*, 1988: 45.
18. *Guinness 1989*, 1988: 49.
19. *Guinness 1989*, 1988: 55.
20. *Guinness 1989*, 1988: 54.
21. *Guinness 1989*, 1988: 55.
22. *Guinness 1989*, 1988: 56.
23. *Guinness 1989*, 1988: 58.
24. *Guinness 1989*, 1988: 61.

25. *Guinness 1989*, 1988: 61.
26. *Guinness 1989*, 1988: 63.
27. *Guinness 1989*, 1988: 63.
28. *Guinness 1989*, 1988: 66.
29. *Guinness 1989*, 1988: 78.
30. *Guinness 1989*, 1988: 38.
31. *Guinness 1989*, 1988: 38.
32. Young, 1985: 11.
33. Cole, 1989: 2.
34. *Guinness 1989*, 1988: 45.
35. Young, 1985: 11.
36. Young, 1985: 11.
37. Cole, 1989: 2.
38. Young, 1985: 11.
39. National Center for Health Statistics, *Advance Report of Final Mortality Statistics*, 1989: 14.
40. Young, 1985: 11.
41. Vierck, 1988: 91.
42. Young, 1985: 11.
43. *Guinness 1989*, 1988: 63.
44. Young, 1985: 11.
45. Young, 1985: 11.
46. Young, 1985: 11.
47. Young, 1985: 11.
48. Young, 1985: 11.
49. Young, 1985: 11.
50. Young, 1985: 11.
51. Young, 1985: 11.
52. Young, 1985: 11.
53. Young, 1985: 11.
54. Young, 1985: 11.
55. Young, 1985: 11.
56. Young, 1985: 11.
57. Vierck, 1988: 91.
58. U.S. Bureau of the Census, *An Aging World*, 1987: vii.
59. U.S. Bureau of the Census, *An Aging World*, 1987: vii.
60. U.S. Bureau of the Census, *An Aging World*, 1987: vii.
61. U.S. Bureau of the Census, *An Aging World*, 1987: vii.
62. U.S. Bureau of the Census, *An Aging World*, 1987: vii.
63. U.S. Bureau of the Census, *An Aging World*, 1987: vii.
64. U.S. Bureau of the Census, *An Aging World*, 1987: vii.
65. The facts in this section are from Vierck, 1988: 64.
66. The facts in this section are from Vierck, 1988: 78–84.
67. *Guinness 1989*, 1988: 284.
68. *Guinness 1989*, 1988: 283.
69. *Guinness 1989*, 1988: 283.
70. *Guinness 1989*, 1988: 285.
71. *Guinness 1989*, 1988: 271.
72. *Guinness 1989*, 1988: 24.

73. *People,* March 12, 1990: 40.
74. *People,* March 12, 1990: 40.
75. *World Almanac,* 1988: 324.
76. *World Almanac,* 1988: 324.
77. *World Almanac,* 1988: 324.
78. *World Almanac,* 1988: 324.
79. *World Almanac,* 1988: 324.
80. *Guinness 1989,* 1988: 399.
81. *Guinness 1989,* 1988: 325.
82. *Guinness 1989,* 1988: 417.
83. *Guinness 1989,* 1988: 417.
84. *Guinness 1989,* 1988: 333.
85. Gildea, 1990: 146.
86. Gildea, 1990: 145.
87. *Guinness 1989,* 1988: 344.
88. *Guinness 1989,* 1988: 349.
89. *Guinness 1989,* 1988: 351.
90. *Guinness 1989,* 1988: 412.
91. *Guinness 1989,* 1988: 412.
92. Parker, 1989: 2A.
93. Parker, 1989: 2A.
94. Parker, 1989: 2A.
95. Parker, 1989: 2A.

Major Legislation Related to Aging

Landmark Legislation from 1930 to 1989

1930	Civil Service Retirement Act
1935	Social Security Act
1937	U.S. Housing Act
1949	Housing Act of 1949
1959	Housing Act of 1959
1964	Urban Mass Transit Act
1965	Medicare and Medicaid
1965	Older Americans Act
1967	Age Discrimination in Employment Act
1972	Equal Employment Opportunity Act
1973	Comprehensive Employment and Training Act
1974	Housing and Community Development Act
1974	Employee Retirement Income Security Act
1976	Energy Conservation and Production Act
1978	Congregate Housing Services Act
1981	Omnibus Budget Reconciliation Act
1983	Social Security Amendments
1986	Amendments to the Age Discrimination in Employment Act
1988	Medicare Catastrophic Coverage Act
1989	Medicare Catastrophic Coverage Act Repeal

National Professional Gerontology Associations

A Dedicated Corps of Gerontologists

Members of the American Society on Aging: 7,000.[1]

Members of the Association for Gerontology in Higher Education: 305 accredited institutions of higher education.[2]

Members of the Gerontological Society of America: 6,500-plus.[3]

Members of the National Association of Area Agencies on Aging: 600 Area Agencies on Aging.[4]

Members of the National Association of State Units on Aging: 57.[5]

Members of the National Caucus and Center on Black Aged: 2,500.[6]

Members of the National Council of the Aging: 6,500.[7]

Members of the National Hispanic Council on Aging: 1,500.[8]

Members of the National Indian Council on Aging: 240.[9]

Notes

1. American Association for International Aging, 1989: 12.
2. American Association for International Aging, 1989: 57.
3. American Association for International Aging, 1989: 71.
4. American Association for International Aging, 1989: 80.
5. American Association for International Aging, 1989: 83.
6. American Association for International Aging, 1989: 84.
7. American Association for International Aging, 1989: 90.
8. American Association for International Aging, 1989: 92.
9. American Association for International Aging, 1989: 224.

Bibliography

Aging Society Project. *Hispanics in an Aging Society.* Fernando Torres-Gil, editor. New York: Carnegie Corporation, 1986.

Alzheimer's Disease: Problems, Prospects, and Perspectives. Harvey J. Altman, editor. New York: Plenum Press, 1987.

American Association for International Aging. *U.S. Directory and Source Book on Aging.* Silver Spring, MD: Business Publishers, Inc., 1989.

American Association of Homes for the Aging. *Provider News* Vol.4, No.1 (January 13, 1989).

American Association of Retired Persons (AARP). *Changing Needs for Long-Term Care.* Washington, DC: IA, Undated.

American Association of Retired Persons (AARP). *Washington Report.* September-October 1989.

American Council of Life Insurance. *1988 Life Insurance Fact Book.* Washington, DC: IA, 1988.

Atlantic Monthly. "The September Almanac." September 1989.

Bausell, R. Barker. "Health Seeking Behavior among the Elderly." *The Gerontologist* Vol.26, No.5 (October 1986).

Bowe, Claudia. "The Up Generation: A Louis Harris Survey for Lear's." *Lear's* Vol.2, No.1 (March 1989).

Brock, D. B., and J. A. Brody. "Statistical and Epidemiological Characteristics." in *Principles of Geriatric Medicine,* R. Andres, E. Bierman, and W. Hazzard, editors. New York: McGraw Hill, 1984.

Brody, Jane E. "The Reality of Elderly Alcoholics and Acting to Help Them." *New York Times,* May 12, 1988.

Carlson, Eugene. "Graying Market May Not Be So Golden." *Wall Street Journal,* December 27, 1989.

Carroll, Ginny. "Growing Old Behind Bars." *Newsweek,* November 20, 1989.

Chambers Associates. "A Summary of 1988 Action of the FY 1989 Federal Budget." Washington, DC: Chambers Associates, November 27, 1989.

Cohen, Mark A., Eileen J. Tell, and Stanley S. Wallack. "The Lifetime Risks and Costs of Nursing Home Use among the Elderly." *Medical Care* Vol.24, No.12 (December 1986).

Cole, Al. "When Is Old?" *NRTA Bulletin* Vol.30, No.6 (June 1989).

Commonwealth Fund Commission on Elderly People Living Alone. *Aging Alone.* Prepared by Judith D. Kasper. New York: IA, 1988.

Conference Board. "The Issues of Public Concern." New York: IA, August 1988.

Conference Board. "Midlife and Beyond." New York: IA, 1985.

Conference Board. "The Public View of Public Spending." New York: IA, March 1988.

Consumer Research Center. *Midlife and Beyond.* New York: IA, 1985.

Daniel Yankelovich Group. *The Mature Americans.* Washington, DC: American Association of Retired Persons, Fall 1987.

Coughlin, Teresa A., and Korbin Liu. "Health Care Costs of Older Persons with Cognitive Impairments." *The Gerontologist* Vol.29, No.2 (April 1989).

Displaced Homemakers Network. *A Status Report on Displaced Homemakers and Single Parents in the United States.* Washington, DC: IA, 1987.

Duncan, Greg J. *Years of Poverty, Years of Plenty: The Changing Economic Fortunes of American Workers and Families.* Michigan: University of Michigan, Institute for Social Research, 1984.

Dychtwald, Ken, and Joe Flower. *Age Wave.* Los Angeles: Tarcher, 1989.

Eicher, Diane. "Health." *Denver Post,* December 18, 1989.

Ettinger, R. *The Prospect of Immortality.* Garden City, NY: McFadden Books, 1964.

Exter, Thomas. "Demographic Forecasts." *American Demographics* April 1989.

Families USA. *The Unaffordability of Nursing Home Insurance.*
Washington, DC: IA, January 1990.

Federal Bureau of Investigation. *Uniform Crime Reports for the
United States.* Washington, DC: IA, 1988.

Fullerton, Howard N. "Labor Force Projections: 1986 to 2000."
Monthly Labor Review, September 1987.

Gibson, Rose Campbell. *Blacks in an Aging Society.* New York:
Carnegie Corporation, July 1986.

Gildea, William. "Winning At Any Age." *Reader's Digest,* February
1990.

Groller, Ingrid. "Caring for Our Parents." *Parents* Vol.64, No.5
(May 1989).

Guinness Book of World Records, 27th Edition. New York: Sterling,
1988.

Harris, Louis. *Inside America.* New York: Random House
(Vintage), 1987.

Harris, Louis. *The Myth and Reality of Aging in America.*
Washington, DC: National Council on Aging, 1975.

Herz, Diane. "Employment Characteristics of Older Women,
1987." *Monthly Labor Review,* September 1988.

Independent Sector. *Giving and Volunteering in the United States.*
Washington, DC: IA, 1988.

International Association for Aging. *U.S. Directory and Source Book
on Aging.* Silver Spring, MD: Business Publishers, Inc., 1989.

Kutscher, Ronald E., and Howard N. Fullerton. "The Aging Labor
Force." Conference on the Aging of the Work Force, Detroit,
Michigan, March 10, 1988.

Lapham, Lewis H., Michael Pollan, and Eric Etheridge. *The
Harper's Index Book.* New York: Henry Holt, 1987.

Longino, Charles F., and William H. Crown. "The Migration of Old
Money," *American Demographics* Vol.11, No.10 (October 1989).

The Long-Term Care Campaign. "Facts about Caregivers."
Washington, DC: IA, 1989.

The Long-Term Care Campaign. *What Is Long-Term Care?*
Washington, DC: IA, 1989.

Louis Harris and Associates. *Problems Facing Elderly Americans Living Alone.* New York: IA, June-July 1986.

McConnell, Charles E. "A Note on the Lifetime Risk of Nursing Homes Residence." *The Gerontologist* Vol.24, No.2 (April 1984).

Mature Market Report. "Fast Facts." Vol.1, No.7 (November 1987).

Mature Market Report. "Fast Facts." Vol.1, No.8 (December 1987).

——. "Uniform Statistics."

Mature Market Report. "Traveling Seniors Broaden Insurance Horizons." Vol.2, No.1 (January 1988).

Mature Market Report. "Dining-Out Patterns Shift with Age." Vol.2, No.2 (February 1988).

Mature Market Report. "Fast Facts." Vol.2, No.3 (March 1988).

——. "Seniors Showcase Awards."

Mature Market Report. "Caveat Venditor: Seller Beware." Vol.2, No.4 (April 1988).

——. "Fast Facts: Mature Americans Study Released."

——. "Media Usage: 50-Plus Consumers as Percentage of Viewers."

Mature Market Report. "Fast Facts." Vol.2, No.5 (May 1988).

——. "Marketers Don't Understand Seniors."

Mature Market Report. "New Research on Senior Spending." Vol.2, No.6 (June 1988).

Mature Market Report. "Fast Facts." Vol.2, No.7 (July 1988).

——. "Over-50 Go to the Movies."

——. "Prevention Study of Home Medical Tests."

——. "Seniors Like Supermarkets."

Mature Market Report. "Automobiles: What Drives Senior Buyers?" Vol.2, No.8 (August 1988).

Mature Market Report. "Acquisitions Shouldn't Lose Seniors." Vol.2, No.9 (September 1988).

——. "Fast Facts."

Mature Market Report. "Senior Travel Up 10 Percent in 1987." Vol.2, No.12 (December 1988).

————. "Seniors Unhappy with Advertising."

Mature Market Report. "Hot on Cold." Vol.3, No.1 (January 1989).

Mature Market Report. "Cleaning Up." Vol.3, No.2 (February 1989).

————. "Fast Facts."

————. "Seniors: $13 Billion Slice of Food Pie."

Mature Market Report. "British Airways Privileged Traveler." Vol.3, No.3 (March 1989).

————. "Home Care Facts."

————. "RV Facts."

Mature Market Report. "Fast Facts." Vol.3, No.4 (April 1989).

————. "Senior Segment's Response to Business."

Mature Market Report. "Fast Facts." Vol.3, No.5 (May 1989).

Mature Market Report. "Dental Health." Vol.3, No.6 June/July 1989.

————. "Eldercare Growing Corporate Issue."

————. "Seniors Who Travel May Be Happier."

Mature Market Report. "Fast Facts." Vol.3, No.7 (August/September 1989).

————. "Senior Golfers."

Mature Outlook. "Mileposts." July/August 1988.

McCord, Colin, and Herald P. Freeman. "Excess Mortality in Harlem." *New England Journal of Medicine,* January 18, 1990.

Mercer, Susan O. *Elder Suicide: A National Survey of Prevention and Intervention Programs.* Washington, DC: American Association of Retired Persons, April 1989.

Moody, Harry. *The Abundance of Life: Human Development Policies for an Aging Society.* New York: Columbia University Press, 1988.

Nassif, Janet Zhun. "There's Still No Place Like Home." *Generations* Vol.11, No.2 (Winter 1986–87).

National Center for Health Statistics. *Adult Health Practices in the United States and Canada.* Hyattsville, MD: IA, May 1988. (Comparative and International Vital and Health Statistics Reports, Series 5, No.3)

National Center for Health Statistics. *Advance Report of Final Mortality Statistics, 1987*. Hyattsville, MD: IA, September 26, 1989. (Monthly Vital Statistics Report, Vol.38, No.5)

National Center for Health Statistics. *Aging in the Eighties, Age 65 Years and Over—Use of Community Services*. By Robyn Stone. Hyattsville, MD: IA, September 30, 1986. (Advance Data, No.124)

National Center for Health Statistics. *Current Estimates from the National Health Interview Survey, United States, 1987*. Hyattsville, MD: IA, September 1988. (Vital and Health Statistics, Series 10, No.166)

National Center for Health Statistics. *Current Estimates from the National Health Interview Survey, United States, 1988*. Hyattsville, MD: IA, October 1989. (Vital and Health Statistics, Series 10, No.173)

National Center for Health Statistics. *Discharges from Nursing Homes: Preliminary Data from the 1985 National Nursing Home Survey*. By Edward S. Sekscenski. Hyattsville, MD: IA, September 30, 1987. (Advance Data, No.142)

National Center for Health Statistics. *Health: United States 1988*. Hyattsville, MD: IA, March 1989.

National Center for Health Statistics. *Health Statistics on Older Persons. Analytical and Epidemiological Studies*. By Robert J. Havlick and others. Hyattsville, MD: IA, 1987. (Series 3, No.25)

National Center for Health Statistics. *Smoking and Other Tobacco Use: United States, 1987*. Hyattsville, MD: IA, September 1989. (Data From the National Health Interview Survey, Series 10, No.169)

National Center for Health Statistics. *Use of Dental Services and Dental Health, United States, 1986*. Hyattsville, MD: IA, October 1988. (Data from the National Health Interview Survey, Series 10, No.165)

National Center for Health Statistics. *Use of Nursing Homes by the Elderly: Preliminary Data from the 1985 National Nursing Home Survey*. By Esther Hing. Hyattsville, MD: IA, May 14, 1987. (Advance Data, No.135)

National Center for Health Statistics. *Utilization of Short-Stay Hospitals, United States, 1985, Annual Summary*. Hyattsville, MD: IA, June 1988. (Vital and Health Statistics, Series 13, No.96)

National Council of La Raza. *The Hispanic Elderly: A Demographic Profile.* Prepared by Herminia L. Cubillos and Margarita M. Prieto. Washington, DC: IA, October 1987.

National Institute on Aging. *Answers about Aging: The Aging Man.* Bethesda, MD: IA, Undated.

National Institute on Aging. *Answers about Aging: The Aging Woman.* Bethesda, MD: IA, Undated.

National Institute on Aging. *Answers about Aging: Bones.* By B. Lawrence Riggs. Bethesda, MD: IA, July 1988.

National Institute on Aging. *Answers about Aging: The Heart.* By Jerome L. Fleg. Bethesda, MD: IA, July 1988.

National Institute on Aging. *Answers about Aging: The Psyche.* By Robert N. Butler. Bethesda, MD: IA, July 1988.

National Institute on Aging. *Answers about Aging: Why Women Outlive Men.* By William R. Hazzard. Bethesda, MD: IA, July 1988.

National Institute on Aging. "News Notes." November 9, 1989.

National Institute on Aging. *Special Report on Aging 1988–1989.* Bethesda, MD: IA, 1988.

New Choices. "The Single Life: You're Not Alone." May 1989.

Older Americans Reports. "Myths of Aging Block Progress in Meeting Needs of Elderly." Vol.10, No.46 (November 21, 1986).

Older Americans Reports. "NCHS Survey of Physical Job Abilities Shows Most Persons 55 to 74 Could Perform Work." Vol.11, No.22 (May 29, 1987).

Older Americans Reports. "Briefs." Vol.11, No.23 (June 5, 1987).

Older Americans Reports. "Survey Finds Senior Citizens Confused about Medicare Benefits." Vol.11, No.28 (July 10, 1987).

Older Americans Reports. "Number of Displaced Homemakers Has More than Doubled since 1976." Vol.11, No.32 (August 7, 1987).

Older Americans Reports. "New Data on Elderly." Vol.11, No.47 (November 27, 1987).

Older Americans Reports. "Crimes against Elderly Down, Justice Department Reports." Vol.11, No.48 (December 4, 1987).

Older Americans Reports. "News Briefs." Vol.12, No.14 (April 1, 1988).

Older Americans Reports. "News Briefs." Vol.12, No.16 (April 15, 1988).

Older Americans Reports. "Report on Elderly Living Arrangements Finds Decline in Extended Family Living." Vol.12, No.18 (April 29, 1988).

Older Americans Reports. "Slants and Trends." Vol.12, No.26 (June 24, 1988).

Older Americans Reports. "Most Maine Residents Lack Information or Misunderstand Long-Term Care Services." Vol.12, No.43 (October 28, 1988).

———. "Plight of Chronic Care Workers Tied into Long-Term Care Picture."

Older Americans Reports. "News Briefs." Vol.12, No.46 (November 18, 1988).

Older Americans Reports. "Nearly Half of Elderly Would Be Poor without Social Security." Vol.13, No.1 (January 6, 1989).

Older Americans Reports. "Middle-Aged and Elderly Uncertain about True Costs of Retirement." Vol.13, No.8 (February 24, 1989).

Older Americans Reports. "RSVP Will Have 402,200 Volunteers, Action Director Tells Congress." Vol.3, No.14 (April 7, 1989).

Older Americans Reports. "Poor Households Spend 30% of Income on Housing, CBPP Report Says." Vol.13, No.16 (April 21, 1989).

Older Americans Reports. "Census Reports 17.9% of Elderly Received Some Public Assistance." Vol.13, No.18 (May 5, 1989).

Older Americans Reports. "News Briefs." Vol.13, No.19 (May 12, 1989).

Older Americans Reports. "State and Local News." Vol.13, No.34 (August 25, 1989).

Older Americans Reports. "State and Local News." Vol.13, No.36 (September 15, 1989).

Older Americans Reports. "State and Local News." Vol.13, No.43 (November 3, 1989).

Older Americans Reports. "News Briefs." Vol.13, No.49 (December 19, 1989).

Older Americans Reports. "210,000 Residents Live in 700 CCRCs in the U.S., New AAHA Report Says." Vol.13, No.50 (December 22, 1989).

Older Americans Reports. "Commonwealth Fund Launches Effort To Change Views about Older Workers." Vol.14, No.4 (January 26, 1990).

Older Americans Reports. "Majority of Americans See Need For More Subsidized Senior Housing." Vol.14, No.13 (March 30, 1990).

Otten, Alan L. "People Patterns." *Wall Street Journal,* November 28, 1989.

Parker, Suzy. "USA Snapshots: Tasks Done over a Lifetime." *USA Today,* October 9, 1989.

Parker, Suzy. "USA Snapshots: Mandatory Retirement." *USA Today,* January 22, 1990.

People. "Psychologist Stanley Coren's Bad News Comes Out of Left Field—Lefties Lead Riskier, Shorter Lives." Vol.32, No.19 (November 6, 1989).

People. "Oscar Odds and Ends." Vol.33, No.10 (March 12, 1990).

Peterson, Karen. "Financial Future Bleak for Many Young Women." *USA Today,* December 27, 1989.

Peterson, Karen. "Most Elderly Don't Make Housing Plans." *USA Today,* April 5, 1990.

Pillemer, Karl, and David Finkelhor. "The Prevalence of Elder Abuse: A Random Sample Survey." *The Gerontologist,* Vol. 28, No. 1 (February, 1988).

Pillemer, Karl, and David W. Moore. "Abuse of Patients in Nursing Homes: Findings from a Survey of Staff." *The Gerontologist* Vol.29, No.3 (June 1989).

Pisarsky, A. *Commuting in America.* Westport, CT.: Eno Foundation for Transportation, Inc., 1988.

Seib, Gerald F., and Alan Murray. "Bush Gets Bad Marks for Avoiding Hard Issues." *Wall Street Journal,* November 8, 1989.

Senior Edition USA. "Update." October 1989.

Senior Edition USA. "Update." December 1989.

Soldo, Beth J., and Emily M. Agree. *America's Elderly*. Washington, DC: Population Reference Bureau, 1988.

Soldo, Beth J., and Kenneth G. Manton. "The Graying of America: Demographic Challenges for Socioeconomic Planning." *The Journal of Socioeconomic Planning Sciences,* Vol.19, No.4 (1985).

Stephens, Ray. "New Hurdles at Work." *NRTA Bulletin,* Vol.30, No.11 (December 1989).

Stinson, Frederick, Mary C. Dufour, and Darryl Bertolucci. "Alcohol-Related Morbidity in the Aging Population," Epidemiological Bulletin No.20, *Alcohol Health and Research World.* 1989.

Transamerica Life Companies. "2 Generations View Their Financial Futures." Los Angeles: IA, July 1988.

Transportation Research Board, National Research Council. *Transportation in an Aging Society.* Special Report 218. Washington, DC: IA, 1988.

U.S. Bureau of the Census. *Aging in the Third World.* By Kevin Kinsella. Washington, DC: IA, 1988.

U.S. Bureau of the Census. *An Aging World.* By Barbara Boyle Torrey, Kevin Kinsella, and Cynthia M. Taeuber. Washington, DC: IA, September 1987.

U.S. Bureau of the Census. *America's Centenarians.* Washington, DC: IA, June 1987.

U.S. Bureau of the Census. *Computer Use in the United States: 1984.* By Robert Kominski. Washington, DC: IA, March 1988 (Current Population Reports, Special Studies, Series P-23, No.155)

U.S. Bureau of the Census. *Demographic and Socioeconomic Aspects of Aging in the United States.* Washington, DC: IA, August 1984. (Current Population Reports, Series P-23, No.138)

U.S. Bureau of the Census. *Educational Attainment in the United States: March 1987 and 1986.* By Robert Kominski. Washington, DC: IA, August 1988. (Current Population Reports, Series P-20, No.428)

U.S. Bureau of the Census. *Historical Statistics of the United States, Colonial Times to 1957.* Washington, DC: IA, 1960.

U.S. Bureau of the Census. *Households, Families, Marital Status, and Living Arrangements: March 1989,* Washington, DC: IA, November 1989. (Current Population Reports, Series P-20, No.441)

U.S. Bureau of the Census. *Marital Status and Living Arrangements, March 1988.* Washington, DC: IA, January 1989. (Current Population Reports, Series P-20, No.433)

U.S. Bureau of the Census. *Money Income of Households, Families, and Persons in the United States, 1987.* Washington, DC: IA, February 1989. (Current Population Reports, Series P-60, No.162)

U.S. Bureau of the Census. *Money Income of Households, Families, and Persons in the United States, 1988.* Washington, DC: IA, October 1989. (Current Population Reports, Series P-60, No.166)

U.S. Bureau of the Census. *Projections of the Population of the United States, by Age, Sex, and Race: 1988 to 2080.* By Gregory Spencer. Washington, DC: IA, January 1989. (Current Population Reports, Series P-25, No.1018)

U.S. Bureau of the Census. *State Population and Household Estimates, With Age, Sex, and Components of Change: 1981–87.* Washington, DC: IA, May 1988. (Current Population Reports, Series P-25, No.1024)

U.S. Bureau of the Census. *Statistical Abstract of the United States, 1988.* Washington, DC: IA, December 1987.

U.S. Bureau of the Census. *Statistical Abstract of the United States, 1989.* Washington, DC: IA, January 1989.

U.S. Department of Commerce and U.S. Department of Housing and Urban Development. *American Housing Survey for the United States in 1985.* Washington, DC: IA, December 1988. (Current Housing Reports, H-150-85)

U.S. Department of Health and Human Services. *Databook on the Elderly: A Statistical Portrait.* By Michelle Adler, Suzanne Kitchen, and Albert Irion. Washington, DC: IA, June 1987.

U.S. Department of Health and Human Services. *Medicaid Medical Vendor Payments by Basis of Eligibility or Receipient and by Region and State,* July 15, 1988. Unpublished.

U.S. Department of Health and Human Services. *Surgeon General's Workshop, Health Promotion and Aging.* Faye G. Abdellah and Steven R. Moore, editors. Washington, DC: IA, March 20–23, 1988.

U.S. Department of Labor, Bureau of Labor Statistics. *Employment and Earnings.* Washington, DC: IA, January 1989.

U.S. Department of Labor, Bureau of Labor Statistics. *Labor Market Problems of Older Workers.* Washington, DC: IA, January 1989.

U.S. House of Representatives, Committee on Ways and Means. *Background Material and Data on Programs within the Jurisdiction of the Committee on Ways and Means.* Washington, DC: IA, 1989.

U.S. Senate Special Committee on Aging in conjunction with the American Association of Retired Persons, the Federal Council on Aging, and the U.S. Administration on Aging. *Aging America: Trends and Projections.* 1987–88 Edition. Washington, DC: IA, 1987.

U.S. Senate Special Committee on Aging. *Aging America: Trends and Projections.* Updated by Elizabeth Vierck. Washington, DC: IA. November 1989.

U.S. Senate Special Committee on Aging. *Developments in Aging 1987: Volume 3.* Washington, DC: IA, 1988.

U.S. Senate Special Committee on Aging. *Developments in Aging 1988: Volume 2.* Washington, DC: IA, 1989.

U.S. Senate Special Committee on Aging. "Revamping Rural Health Care." *Aging Reports.* Spring-Summer 1989.

USA Today. "Your Retirement Fund Is Safe and Growing." October 9, 1989.

USA Today. "Briefly." November 21, 1989.

United Way of America. *Retirees as Volunteers.* Alexandria, VA: IA, 1988.

University of California, "Fascinating Facts." *Berkeley Wellness Letter,* Vol.5, No.11 (August 1989).

Veterans Administration. *Veteran Population September 30, 1988.* Washington, DC: IA, October 1988.

Vierck, Elizabeth. *Older Is Better.* Washington, DC: Acropolis Books, 1988.

Villers Foundation. *On the Other Side of Easy Street.* Washington, DC: IA, January 1987.

Waldo, Daniel R., Sally T. Sonnefeld, David R. McKusick, and Ross H. Arnett. "Health Expenditures by Age Group: 1977 and 1987." *Health Care Financing Review* Vol.10, No.4 (September 1989).

Walz, Thomas, Dennis Harper, and John Wilson. "The Aging Developmentally Disabled Person: A Review." *The Gerontologist* Vol.26, No.6 (December 1986).

Ward, Adrienne. "Marketers Slow To Catch Age Wave." *Advertising Age* Vol.60, No.22 (May 22, 1989).

Waterbor, J., P. Cole, E. Delzell, and D. Andjelkovich. "Mortality Experience of Major League Baseball." *New England Journal of Medicine* Vol. 318, No.19 (May 1988).

Weiss, Daniel Evan. *100% American.* New York: Simon and Schuster (Poseidon), 1988.

Weiss, Michael J. *The Clustering of America.* New York: Harper and Row, 1988.

Weinberg, Hedy. "Update." *Senior Edition USA,* March 1989.

Weinberg, Hedy. "Update." *Senior Edition USA,* December 1989.

World Almanac and Book of Facts 1989. New York: Scripps Howard (Pharos Books), 1988.

Young, Gayle. "New Science Studies How—and Why—We Wear Out." *Chicago Tribune,* December 1, 1985.

Index